WIN THE RETIREMENT GAME

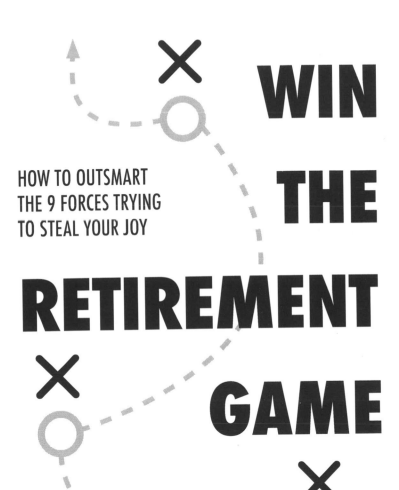

WIN THE

RETIREMENT

GAME

HOW TO OUTSMART
THE 9 FORCES TRYING
TO STEAL YOUR JOY

JOE CASEY

HOUNDSTOOTH
PRESS

WIN THE RETIREMENT GAME

How to Outsmart the 9 Forces Trying to Steal Your Joy

FIRST EDITION

ISBN   978-1-5445-3276-9   *Hardcover*

         978-1-5445-3275-2   *Paperback*

         978-1-5445-3277-6   *Ebook*

*To my wife Pat, and Sarah, Sean, Joanna, Rebecca,
Matt, and our new granddaughter, Sloane*

CONTENTS

INTRODUCTION

Early retirement had long been Jim's dream, and at fifty-nine, he was four years into living it. He'd done everything right—or so he thought. He had saved and invested well. He and wife Helen had meticulously managed their expenses. He smiled, remembering the day their financial planner told them he could retire early, at fifty-five, exactly as they had planned. They had achieved financial independence.

Now, with freedom from work, Jim was time rich as well. As he looked out at the brilliant green of the park adjacent to their home, Jim realized he and Helen had the life they had always wanted. But something was missing. Yes, they were relishing the flexibility to do whatever they pleased, whenever they wanted. They were traveling frequently, playing their fill of golf and tennis, and making up for lost time with family and friends.

But for the last year, Jim had been feeling out of sorts, even a little down. He felt empty, rudderless, and, he finally admitted to himself, bored. The things he had looked forward to for so many years were losing their luster. And he knew that at his age, God willing, he probably had many more years of retirement ahead. On this sunny perfect day, the thought came to him clearly: "I can't keep living this way for the rest of my life."

He felt stuck, and suddenly he was afraid about his future.

Helen had noticed, and as Jim gazed out their large picture window, she said, "Maybe you miss working more than you thought you would. Are you thinking about going back to work?"

"I've thought about that. I don't want to jump back on the merry-go-round again, though I wouldn't mind hearing the music play every once in a while," said Jim. "But I'm not sure what I could do part-time after being away for four years."

Jim's scenario is far too common. Many people discover their money is better prepared for retirement than they are. It's easy to think of planning for retirement as solely a financial matter. Financial planning takes a certain mindset. It's a left-brain process. It's quantitative, linear, and logical. It takes discipline. Risks are to be managed.

However, many people who are well-prepared financially fail to plan as well for how they'll invest their most valuable asset—their time. It's easy to put off, and it may require stepping out of their comfort zone. Planning for how you'll live your future life takes a different mindset. It's a right-brain process. It's qualitative, non-linear, and intuitive. It takes imagination. Risks are to be explored.

Retirement today is likely totally different than when you first joined the workforce. For most people, it's much longer, lasting twenty or even thirty years or more. And it frequently comes earlier than expected, with almost half of American retirees reporting that they retired earlier than planned, an average of five years earlier.[1]

Retirement now often includes some form of "work," such as a part-time job, consulting, volunteering, or creative endeavors. But the most significant change is that retirement is being *reframed*. Retirement used to be viewed as a period of withdrawal and decline. Now it's seen as being a period of renewal, engagement, meaningful pursuits, and personal growth. Such change requires a whole new approach to retirement planning, one that addresses the emotional aspects and helps you get smarter about aging well.

The pandemic raised the stakes. People have a keener appreciation for what matters most, and they want more from their remaining years. They want those years to have meaning.

With balanced planning, you can enter retirement better prepared. But that's only part of the story. As the saying goes, *Man plans, and God laughs*. Retirement is full of surprises. Some appear right away; others emerge over time. And the nonfinancial challenges that pop up stand squarely between you and a fulfilling life in retirement, that is until you defeat them.

This book will introduce you to the nine opponents people meet when they retire. They may not be what you expect. Some adversaries, like Boredom, the Status Quo, and Inertia, appear innocuous, yet are pernicious. The effects of other antagonists—like the paralysis of Uncertainty, the isolation of Loneliness, and the weight of other people's Expectations—are more readily apparent. Finally, the disorientation of Overwhelm, the gravity of Obligations, and Drifting without direction can derail your retirement dreams in the end.

To conquer these foes, you'll learn how to size up each one and craft a different strategy to target its specific weaknesses. Each opponent ultimately wilts when confronted by its particular "Kryptonite," and you'll learn the research-based formula for each. You'll discover how you can add the right tools to your retirement arsenal by sparking Curiosity, embracing Change, cultivating Connectivity, unleashing Creativity, welcoming Acceptance, gaining Clarity, seeking Challenge, discerning a Calling, and unlocking a new Purpose.

HOW I CAN HELP

I'm an executive coach who also helps successful people design their new lives after full-time work. It gives me a rare front-row seat to the battles people grapple with in building new lives with greater meaning and purpose. It's a journey I've traveled myself, having taken early retirement at fifty-two to pursue a second career. This work inspired me to go back to school to complete a Masters in Gerontology (at sixty) to understand the research on how to age well. I wrote this book to take you inside the challenges my clients face, so you will be prepared and can tap into research-based solutions to help you develop your unique next life.

This book is *not* for retirees who want to just kick back and relax in retirement. There's nothing wrong with that—it's a vital part of this next phase of life. But for some, that's not enough. This book is for the people who want to enjoy life, but who also want *more* out of life after their full-time careers. It's for people who aren't done just yet and know they have more left in the tank. It's for people who are curious about how their skills, experience, and wisdom can be redirected in new ways to benefit others while preserving the flexibility "retirement" promises.

It's also for the retiree who's looking for an upgrade when retirement isn't what they expected. It's for the one who's comfortably nestled in first class in their financial life but feels stuck in a middle seat in coach in their day-to-day life. It's for the couple who hasn't talked about their hopes and concerns about retirement but who know they should. It's for the reader who's been forced to retire earlier than expected and needs to figure out a new path forward.

Back to Jim. Over the next year, he pivoted and created a new portfolio of interests adding one building block at a time. He landed a part-time (and lower key) version of work, teaching financial literacy to community college students, repurposing the knowledge gained over his career in finance. Next, Jim reclaimed a pastime he had given up, joining a bicycling club, which led to a new set of friends, all while keeping himself in great shape. He accepted a role on the board of a local organization whose mission he cares about and volunteered to start a new program helping underprivileged youth. He also began taking classes on topics he was always curious about but never had time to explore, including a series of cooking classes. Now he's working toward becoming something of a self-described "gourmet chef" at home, although Helen remains skeptical about that.

Best of all, Jim and Helen still find time to do many of the things they both enjoy together. "I'm still having my share of fun," he said, "but it's no longer the only thing on my schedule. I have a diverse mix now, and the things I'm pursuing are meaningful to me and to others. I'm giving back, but I'm also learning so much along the way. I never found my new purpose, but I have something better—a multipurpose retirement."

Now that you've heard how Jim's story turned out, let me introduce you to another character. I want to take you on a journey with Pete, who is not a real person but an amalgamation of the dozens of clients I've worked with over the past seven years.

This book tells the story of Pete's journey to illustrate the challenges you too could face, so you can anticipate them. None of my clients wrestle with all nine of the opponents I've listed above. But Pete's a brave soul, and he's taking on all of them for your benefit.

Pete's in his mid-fifties and in the midst of a busy, successful career. Sometimes, following a hectic period at work, he steps back and wonders what his life will be like someday without work. Today is one of those days. As he enters his home office, he's fantasizing about it. But it scares him a little. As he checks his calendar, he muses, *What exactly would I do without work? Who would I BE without work?*

CHAPTER ONE

WELCOME TO THE RETIREMENT GAME

"It's not what happens to you, but how you react to it that matters."

—EPICTETUS

As Pete waited for the others to join the first Zoom call of his day, he reflected on how grateful he was for his work life. His promotion five years earlier to regional director put him in the perfect role. It fully leveraged his strengths. It was challenging work, but challenging in the right way. It brought out the best in him. Pete had built a strong team, an all-star roster that was the envy of his peers. He enjoyed helping his best people become even better and mature as leaders. It came with managing competing egos, but he was used to that. Big egos were everywhere he turned. It was usually more amusing than troubling, although there were some tense moments. But all in all, he loved his job.

In his personal life, Pete was happy. His relationship with his wife, Melissa, seemed to get better every year. They had the typical struggles every dual-career couple faces, but they had learned how to make it work. Their two children were doing well. It was hard for Pete to believe, but their daughter Anne was already in her sophomore year of college, and their son Andy was headed to college in the fall. They would suddenly be empty nesters. Where had the time gone?

As the pandemic spread, Pete jumped into crisis management mode. He wasn't the work-from-home type, but he quickly adjusted to operating from his home office. The days blurred together in a haze of videoconferences. Zoom-land. All day. Every day.

Pete was grateful he and his family members were all healthy, but at work, he started to become concerned about the numbers. Yet, his boss and the company's top leadership remained steadfastly optimistic. Pete listened carefully as they emphasized the company's financial strength and touted the resilience shown during previous crises.

Still, something was bothering Pete. The public pronouncements and private conversations sounded precisely the same. *That* was unusual. His boss and other senior people he had known for years would often confide in him and share valuable intel on what was actually happening. "Look, strictly between us, here's the deal" is the way those conversations would begin. This time, though, it felt like the *Invasion of the Body Snatchers*. Everyone was "on message" 24/7, reading from the same script in unison. *Well, maybe they're just confident we'll be able to gut this out*, Pete thought.

He got the call early on a Friday afternoon. His boss, John, would sometimes call at that time to check in informally, but this time, his tone was different.

"Peter (he had never once called him that), we're selling the business to Mega Corp. It will be announced right after the market closes today. Mega Corp's regional directors will be taking over immediately. Your position, along with the other regional directors here, is being eliminated, effective today. Today will be your last day with the company. Your severance package and outplacement will begin on Monday. I'm transferring you now to Megan in HR. She'll explain the details."

"But, John, hold on a sec..."

"Pete, I'm sorry about this, but here's Megan," said John. "Thank you for your service."

Pete looked down at his phone. His call with his boss John lasted thirty-two seconds. Pete had worked for the company for sixteen years. Two seconds per year?

Pete was too stunned to hear most of what Megan had to say. He took a few notes on the tangible facts he could discern from the torrent of HR jargon. He'd receive one year of severance. Benefits coverage followed by COBRA. Eligibility for early retirement. Outplacement counseling from a company to help him find another job.

Pete took a long walk to try and process what had happened. As he sorted things out, he tallied up the opportunities and the challenges. He had a year to work with to figure out what he wanted to do next. Pete and Melissa were planners, and they had invested and lived conservatively. They were in good shape financially.

The challenge was what to do next. He had no clue. Nada.

Pete's next step was a thirty-minute Zoom call with Jason, his outplacement counselor. Jason was friendly and upbeat. He outlined his agenda. His goals were to orient Pete on how the outplacement process worked and to get him "pumped up for his next job."

Jason's list took twenty-five minutes. He then explained what would be required from Pete in the outplacement process. Jason confided that his "caseload" was up to forty-two people, and so their one-on-one Zoom calls would need to be highly efficient. He explained the reports he needed to generate each week on Pete's activity. Pete would need to hit all the milestones, or Jason would be in hot water. Then he faced the camera with a sincere look and asked Pete, "So, what are *your* goals?"

Pete began to explain. He was pretty sure he didn't want a new job. He thought this was the chance to achieve his dream of early retirement, albeit a bit earlier than he expected. But he wasn't sure about that yet either. Jason interrupted and apologized. It was time for his next Zoom call. "Ciao, Pete."

Pete reached out to Tom, Megan's boss in HR. They went back a long way. Pete expected it would be tough to get Tom, given how busy he'd be on the merger integration. But Tom took Pete's call right away. Pete explained, "I need your help. I think I need a different outplacement counselor. Do you have any pull with this outplacement company?"

"Hold on," Tom said. "Tell me what's going on and what you're thinking about doing next." After a while, Tom added, "You don't need them. I know a guy who can help you. Let me connect the two of you."

A REAL COACH

Meeting Rick, the coach Tom recommended, was a completely different experience from Pete's call with Jason. Rick started with a series of thought-provoking questions. He asked about what had happened, how Pete felt about it, and what his priorities were now. Pete told him he was seriously thinking about early retirement, but he wasn't sure what he would *do*. Retiring seemed appealing, but he wasn't sure he was ready to take the plunge yet. Rick listened intently. After thirty minutes of questions, Rick asked if he could share a few things he had learned about retirement.

Rick explained that Pete—and Pete alone—would decide what success meant in this next phase of life. "Pete, when you're graduating from the world of full-time work, you'll need to create a new scorecard. You've got to define what winning will be for you now. Only you can decide that. What most people have in common is they want these last chapters in life to be meaningful. It will be different for each person. But to win the Retirement Game, just like any game, you'll have to beat some opponents along the way. Some people who aren't well prepared don't know who their opponents are until they're face-to-face with them in retirement. They're surprised, shocked, even. And then they struggle. It doesn't have to be that way," said Rick. "Pete, you can prepare for them and have a game plan for each one."

OPEN TO REINVENTION

Rick pointed out that many people fail to see the transition to retirement as a significant life event. Many people don't realize it's one of the ten most stressful ones you'll encounter in life, according to The American Institute of Stress's Holmes-Rahe Stress Inventory.[1] It demands you adapt to new realities, and a lot of things change when you leave your job.

People enter retirement at different ages and with various levels of resources. But all new retirees are *time rich*. The question is: How will you invest that time? Conservatively, most retirees have 2,500 hours each year formerly dedicated to full-time work, now free to allocate any way they like.[2]

New retirees view those 2,500 hours differently. There are some who look at those 2,500 hours as a problem (*How will I possibly fill all that time?*) whereas others see them as an opportunity (*I have so many ideas and things I want to do. How can I possibly choose?*).

As Rick explained to Pete, "There's loss when you leave the workplace. Some losses are obvious right off the bat. Others creep up on you. But at one point or another, you'll feel a sense of loss. For example, most people describe themselves by what they do for a living. Once that's gone, the question becomes, Who am I *now*? There's also a loss of the structure to your days, weeks, months, and years that work gave you. For many people, especially men, there's a loss of social contact and camaraderie when they move away from full-time work. Finally, there's a loss of purpose. What's the driving force for me *now*?

"But don't worry, Pete. There are plenty of gains, too. The biggest one is that now you have freedom. What will you do with it?"

CREATING A NEW STORY

"Some people fall into the trap of thinking retirement equals vacation," Rick said. "It's so easy to slip into vacation mode. However, after a while, some people realize vacation mode is not well suited for the length of retirement today, and they want more out of life. Other people get stuck on the losses I mentioned. They end up living in the past, consumed by anger, resentment, or regret. They're done with work, and work is done with them. You can see it in their eyes. They're kind of done with life, too. And they drift."

Rick paused.

"Arc *you* done, Pete?" he asked.

"With work? I think so. Well, maybe. With life? Ah, no. Definitely not," said Pete.

"Then my mission is to help you build a new story—a new narrative on what's next for you. It's a story that starts with the reality of where you are now," said Rick. "It progresses by exploring what's possible, then going through a series of experiments to discover the right path for you. It's the next chapter of your life story.

"Your story doesn't end with Mega Corp," said Rick. "It's a pivot point. This opens up new options and possibilities. It may be unclear right now, but you've got the pen. Writing the next chapter is up to you."

OPEN TO A NEW IDENTITY

"And remember, Pete, you're dealing with this all of a sudden. When you're forced to retire earlier than you planned, you're thrust into the deep end of the pool," said Rick. "So, be kind to yourself.

"Those losses I mentioned are real. You'll feel them intensely. But over time, you'll address them by replacing the things you got from work beyond the paycheck. A new purpose. A new structure and rhythm to your days. And a new answer to the question: So, what do you do?

"Some people answer that question in the past tense. They describe who they used to be. But people who are thriving in this next chapter answer it differently, in the present tense. They describe what they're engaged in, what drives them now. They talk about the new story they're living.

"Now, it takes some time," continued Rick, "but they let go and move on to something new. Sometimes it includes some form of work, and sometimes it doesn't. The key is that you let go of being tied to what you used to do. You can't move forward until you do.

"That doesn't mean abandoning what you used to do. It can mean repurposing your skills and experience in new ways. Exploring different ways, you can redirect your time and talents to help others," said Rick.

THE IMPORTANCE OF ATTITUDE

"Another differentiator is the attitude people bring to retirement. Those who thrive are optimistic, yet realistic. They are clear-eyed about what they can't control but excited about what they can. They're open-minded about their future. And they take ownership. They have a strong belief that their actions can create the future they desire. They are active, not passive. But they're not frenetic either. Above all, they have a sense of humor that gives them perspective," said Rick.

"The people who struggle have a different mindset. They concentrate more on the problems than the opportunities. They're more insular. They stick more with what and who they already know, even though those circles are getting smaller. They have a pessimistic view of the future. They get stuck. They have a narrow field of vision.

"Your new story will begin with your initial vision of your future, Pete," Rick said. "It will get more specific over time. It's funny. When we're kids, it's easy to dream. Ask any kid what they want to be when they grow up, and you'll get a great answer! So, you get another chance to dream a bit. Now that you *are* grown up, we'll talk about who you want to be next."

"Well, I should warn you. I'm not much of a dreamer," said Pete.

"That's okay. We won't stay very long in Dreamland. You need much more than a vision," said Rick. "We'll be dealing with the opponents who want to steal your joy in retirement."

GAME ON

"You keep mentioning opponents," said Pete. "I'm thinking of *retiring*. Facing opponents sounds too much like *work*."

"Sorry to break this to you, but nothing good comes too easy, Pete," said Rick. "The positive things you want in retirement are there for the taking. But you'll have to earn them, just as you did in your working life. For every positive thing you pursue, you'll need to overcome an opposing force pulling you away from it. It'll feel like a tug-of-war sometimes. While you're still working, it's fun to picture life in retirement: a chance to do what you want when you want, the relief of not having to get up and go to work. But it's a mistake to picture retirement as one-dimensional. There's much more to life in retirement than *not* working. A great retirement is multidimensional. Retirement is full of competing opportunities and challenges. There are tensions and paradoxes, many of which you won't expect."

THE OPPOSING FORCES

"Did you ever play sports, Pete?" asked Rick.

"Sure. I played basketball."

"Okay. So, think of retirement as a game. It's a game you want to win. As with any game, you'll face different opponents trying to block you and prevent you from advancing. The opponents are easier in the early going, but they get tougher as you go along. In this game, they're trying to keep you from the life you want."

"Wow. I hadn't thought of retirement that way," said Pete.

Rick took another long pause.

"Do you like challenges, Pete? Do they bring out the best in you?" asked Rick.

"Yes. I think so. But I didn't think I'd face *so many* challenges in retirement."

"Are you a competitive person? In the sense of reaching your potential and becoming the best version of yourself?"

"Absolutely."

"Okay. Then you'll do well with this approach."

BAD IS STRONGER THAN GOOD

Just like Pete, you too will be the underdog against many of these adversaries in the Retirement Game that Rick talks about. Why? Social psychologist Roy Baumeister and his colleagues conducted a meta-analysis of psychological studies and concluded that *Bad is Stronger than Good*.[3] They found that adverse events are more powerful and have longer-lasting consequences than positive ones. They theorize that this phenomenon has an evolutionary basis. For survival, it's critical to be attuned to threats. We learn critical lessons from adverse events so we can avoid them in the future. Baumeister and his colleagues surmised that the negatives serve as a signal for change. They nudge you to invest more effort to move toward what you want.

"Adversaries and underdogs? This is more than I expected," said Pete. "I was thinking of going to the beach for a while or taking golf lessons or a class or something. Maybe start a band?"

"It's up to you," said Rick, followed by another silence.

"Okay. I'm intrigued by this Retirement Game idea. What does it take to win?" asked Pete.

"Well, you'll have a secret weapon you can count on in all of the rounds," said Rick. "It's the 'Power of New.'

"If you're willing to try new things, it gives you a big advantage. When we're learning something new, we have to show up with an open mind. It helps us be more open to learning from our experience. So, we'll start small, test new things, capture the learnings, adjust, then expand from there. You can change behaviors in significant ways by starting with small steps.[4]

"Pete, have you ever known someone who's stuck in a rut?" asked Rick.

"Sure."

"A few years ago, I noticed myself resisting trying something

new," said Rick. "It was a small thing, but it stopped m
my tracks. I was walking down the street with our younge
daughter Rebecca, a college student in Washington, DC. We
were talking about where we should go to dinner. My ideas
were all the tried-and-true favorites. She suggested we try
this Ethiopian restaurant. I made the 'Dad face.' That's when
I realized I wasn't open to trying something new, even something as simple as a new restaurant. We went, and guess what?
It was great.

"The experience reminded me how important it is to keep
trying new things. The best book I've read on retirement
covers this topic. In *Refire! Don't Retire*, Ken Blanchard and
Morton Shaevitz write about The Serendipity Club.[5] They
invented it to provide a new experience each week by trying
a new cuisine or a new restaurant. The only rule in the club
is that when you are invited, you agree to say yes every time.
You have to be committed to experimenting with new things."

One of the Big Five Factors of Personality is Openness to
Experience. Research indicates two things: first, Openness to
Experience is associated with higher levels of life satisfaction
among older adults;[6] second, some aspects of your personality
may shift in later life, and one of those factors is Openness to
Experience.[7] Bringing an open mind to new experiences can
give you an edge as you create your new story.

TAKEAWAYS

1. Retirement is one of life's most stressful events. It's a
    significant life transition and has a big emotional com-
    ponent. Retirees face changes in status, identity, purpose,

and practical challenges, such as structuring their time independently. Preparing for these changes can make the transition much smoother.

2. There are things to bring to your retirement besides your 401(k). A vision for this new phase of your life and a positive attitude can become your most valuable assets.

3. Only you can decide what fulfillment is for you. Define your new scorecard based on what matters most to you.

4. Be open to new experiences. Seek out opportunities to try new things. It will add variety to your life, and you may just develop a new interest and new relationships. You've earned the right to retire, but it doesn't automatically come with wisdom. You have to earn that too, and it begins with being open to new experiences.

As you follow Pete's journey, take time to complete each exercise at the end of each chapter. You'll get the most out of the book by doing so. To start, let's take stock of what you perceive to be the things you'll lose and gain when you retire.

EXERCISE—YOUR RETIREMENT *NON-FINANCIAL* BALANCE SHEET

What losses and gains do you anticipate when you retire or are you experiencing in retirement?

LOSS	GAIN

1. What's one action you can take to mitigate the most ~ical losses?

2. What's one action you can take to amplify the most important gains?

CHAPTER TWO

CULTIVATE CURIOSITY TO BEAT BOREDOM

"The cure for boredom is curiosity. There is no cure for curiosity."

—DOROTHY PARKER

Pete arrived at Rick's office for their first in-person session, not knowing quite what to expect. It was on the second floor of a historic brick building across the street from the university. Pete liked being back in a college town for the afternoon. It had a different vibe from the city he used to work in every day.

Rick greeted Pete warmly and invited him into his office. Pete took in the various photos displayed in the office. At first glance, the images told the story of an active life. Sports. Family events. Travel.

One photo caught Pete's eye. It was of a basketball player shooting a free throw with impeccable form. In the back-

und, he could see people standing, packed in like sardines
eneath the basket at the other end of the court, which was
unusual. *A standing-room only crowd*, Pete mused. It probably
was a big game. You could feel tension from the photo. The
ball was in mid-flight, and the shooter had a look of intense
concentration, as did the spectators who looked on expec-
tantly. Pete wondered if it was a game winner—or maybe a
game loser.

"So, Rick. I was wondering about that basketball photo. Is that
one of your sons?"

Rick laughed. "Oh no. That's an earlier edition of me from a
very long time ago, back in high school. At that point in my
life, basketball was my main focus. It was my first true love."

"Well, did it go in?" asked Pete.

"That shot? I have no idea," Pete laughed. "Well, it probably
did. I did shoot 90 percent from the line back then "

"Back then? Pete asked. "Do you *still* play?"

"Never forget your first true love, Pete. Remember that."

Once they were both seated, Rick got right to the point. "Pete,
I'm thrilled to have the opportunity to help you. Here's how
we'll work together. You win the Retirement Game by com-
pleting cycles that start with Reflection on what matters most,
then taking action, and learning from your experience. Think
of it as a portfolio of experiments. It will lead you to discover
your new path. That's how you create a great new life, one

experiment at a time. But I must warn you. Along the various opponents will pop up and try to defeat you. T work hard to take you off track. You can't let that happen.

"So, let's get started with where you are. When you think about early retirement, what concerns you?"

"Well," said Pete. "I'm unsure, I guess. Unsure about how that will play out."

"In what way?" asked Rick.

"I'm not sure I'll like it. I'm used to a busy, demanding career," answered Pete.

Rick was doing his silence thing again. *Maybe it's some kind of Jedi-mind trick thing*, thought Pete.

It worked. "Well, I guess I'm afraid," Pete blurted out.

"About what?" asked Rick softly.

"I'm afraid I'll be bored. Without work. Without all the people. Without all the action," said Pete.

"Okay. That's where we'll start then," said Rick. "Boredom's your first opponent. I guarantee you can defeat boredom once you know how it works."

henever facing a challenge, I find it helpful to prepare a scouting report," Rick said.

"You mean as a basketball coach would?"

"Exactly. A scouting report to establish a breakdown of each opponent's strengths and weaknesses. Based on those, we can devise a game plan that will help us defeat each opponent. Get used to this approach, because we'll be doing it for each of the opponents you'll face in retirement."

"Surprisingly, there's a lot of research on boredom," continued Rick. "And yes, it's *boring*. Lucky for you, I've gone through it. It's one of the most common fears my clients have about retirement. Here's what you need to know. Boredom is an emotional state you get in when you're not engaged meaningfully in the world.[1] Be forewarned: boredom is tricky. It can sneak up on you in retirement. The shift from the structured life of work to the freedom of retirement can be abrupt. Having so much flexibility feels liberating, but it can be disorienting.

"Boredom is pernicious. For example, it's easy to fall in love with the honeymoon period early in retirement. You suddenly have a ton of free time, without demanding bosses or urgent emails. Every day is *Saturday*! But after a while, it becomes more like *every single day* is Saturday. You get used to kicking back—and maybe too used to it. A long retirement is a terrible thing to waste."

Pete was thinking how every day being Saturday sounded pretty darn good. *That's a problem I can deal with*, he thought.

"You see, Pete," said Rick, "it's like the boiled frog phenomenon. If you put a frog in a pot of water and *gradually* increase the temperature, the frog never notices the change until the point it boils alive. Boredom is like that. Relaxing is great. But overdo it, and you'll find you have less energy, and you can become more anxious and even irritable."

Studies back up what Rick is saying. Left unchecked, boredom can stall the transition to retirement. It can lead to a loss of purpose that may result in profound boredom and negatively affect social relationships. Boredom prods people to seek stimulation, and often in unhealthy ways. Overindulging on TV and social media are common problems, but some people fall into more destructive behaviors such as eating disorders, gambling, and substance abuse.[2]

It can happen fast. A 2019 British survey of over 1,000 retirees found one in four became bored after just one year of retirement. A third reported having more time alone than they expected.[3] While it's tempting to focus on the fact that 75 percent *weren't* bored, for those who do become bored in retirement, it can put a damper on a phase of life they worked and saved for many years to enjoy.

"Make no mistake, Pete. If you get tangled up with boredom, it can hold you back. I remember a time when it looked like boredom would doom one of my client's retirements," said Rick. "In his case, Boredom had a significant advantage. He was in my client's head big time. It was his biggest fear, and it took a while for him to deal with him. Let me tell you the story."

ad just finished recording a podcast and was looking forward to heading home. The phone rang. It was Abby, a regular
listener. But Abby wasn't calling about herself. She said, "My
husband needs you. He just doesn't know it yet. He's dread-
ing retirement. Oh, and by the way, he will hate the idea of
working with a coach."

Dan was an engineer. He was sixty-four and retiring in six
months. When I met Dan, I learned Abby was right. He didn't
think hiring a coach was a great idea. Regardless, we hit it
off. When we turned to the topic of his retirement, his face
changed instantly. He looked paralyzed. Dan confessed he
was terrified of retirement.

"'I've never told anyone this before. I've been all-in on my work
for as long as I can remember. It's intellectually challenging.
But without my career, I'm worried sick that I'll be bored. I
don't have any hobbies. I don't play golf or tennis. I'm not
sure I even have any real interests anymore outside of work.
I'm afraid I'll fall into a routine of watching TV all day and
become a hermit, like my dad did. I fear I'll waste away the
time I have left. And I know I'll deeply regret it."

Dan was a challenging client. At first, nothing worked. He
wasn't kidding. He didn't appear to have any interests besides
work. Going into our third session, I realized the problem
wasn't Dan. It was me.

I was focusing on his future, which was exactly what he was
fearful of. He wasn't ready to tackle that yet. So, I shifted the
focus to his past. We talked about his life, one decade at a

time. Telling his life story brought him new perspectiv
uncovered many things he once loved to do, things he gave
as his responsibilities increased and his free time evaporate

Through our work together, Dan began experimenting by bringing some of these things back one by one to see what they felt like at this stage of his life. The first thing he brought back was date night. Next, he slowly started working out again, with his doctor's blessing. He resumed doing Tai Chi, which he had done in his forties. Next, he started taking trips to the library, rekindling his interest in reading about history and science fiction. Last, remembering how he loved reading to his son when he was young led him to sign up as a volunteer reading to underprivileged children.

By the time he entered retirement, Boredom wasn't Dan's biggest challenge. His biggest challenge was prioritization. He had so many new things going on that he had to work on being disciplined enough to keep the flexibility he wanted. Revisiting his past had helped him go forward. After Dan and I completed our work together, Abby told me, "I can see the difference in his eyes. I have the man I married back again."

NOT ALL BOREDOM IS BAD

"I get it," said Pete. "We all had a good dose of boredom during the pandemic. But I don't know if I want to get involved in a bunch of things. Part of the appeal of retiring early is getting off the hamster wheel. Do I need to replace one hectic life with another in retirement?"

"Good question," said Rick. "It's up to each person to decide the right pace of life is for them in retirement. Many ~~o~~ple prefer to slow down, but some actually want to speed ~~u~~p. Even in an active retirement, some boredom is inevitable. It's a normal part of life. You just need to learn to recognize it. That's because boredom isn't all bad."

Indeed, there's an *upside* to boredom if you use it right.[4] If you're paying attention, boredom can be a valuable signal. It can alert you that you need to change.[5] But boredom is tricky. One of boredom's favorite traps is getting people to go from bored to *busy*. Boredom would love to lure you into jumping onto a brand-new hamster wheel. But here's the thing. Just being busy won't defeat boredom. It's not about being busy.[6]

> Boredom is a state where you're not engaged in things you find meaningful. That's the key to boredom that is so easy to miss. It's about meaning.[7]

The first step in defeating boredom is accepting temporary boredom as a fact of life. Our use of technology today may be making us less tolerant of boredom. People quickly become uncomfortable with a lack of stimulation and automatically reach for their devices.[8] Instead, it's better to use boredom as a catalyst for reflection. Rather than reaching for your phone, think if there's something more purposeful you could do. Or, simply appreciate a period of silence.

WHAT EXACTLY IS CURIOSITY?

"Let's make sure we define our terms," Rick said as he jumped

up to use the whiteboard in his office. "Here's t.
of curiosity that resonates with me":

Curiosity is the recognition, pursuit, and inherent desire to explore nove
challenging, and uncertain events.[9]

Researchers have found that curiosity is associated with higher levels of life satisfaction and well-being.[10] Curiosity can curb boredom and add variety and excitement to your life in retirement. It can spark the discovery of new interests and activities, and even ignite a passion for lifelong learning.

"Pete, do you know people who've *been there and done that*?" asked Rick. "Well, with curiosity, you won't be jaded like them. You'll experience more wonder, intrigue, and even adventure. It can enrich your life."

"Ok. I'm sold on curiosity. Sign me up," said Pete. "But can we go back to the opponent? How does boredom try to beat curiosity?"

"Well, boredom likes to get inside your head to make you anxious. If it senses a whiff of curiosity, it will create some anxiety. Boredom wants you to get distracted. That's because curiosity isn't useful unless you act," said Rick.[11]

In fact, with curiosity, it's hard to be bored for long. You'll discover new interests that may evolve into a new sense of purpose. Curiosity can even assist you with your relationships, especially your most important ones. If you're genuinely curi-

ther people, you'll ask the right questions, and e people a chance to fulfill one of the greatest human —the need to be understood.[12]

Curiosity helps you keep things interesting in a marriage or other serious relationships, especially if you engage in new experiences and activities together.[13] But make no mistake, curiosity is not a superficial tactic. You have to be genuinely interested.

WHAT'S BLOCKING YOUR VISION?

"Suppose I'm just not a curious person. How do I get more curiosity?" Pete asked.

Rick paused and said, "Pete, when was the last time you stepped back and examined your beliefs?" The question surprised Pete, but he responded, "Well, I believe in God if that's what you're getting at."

"I'm talking about something different. Can I tell you another short story?" asked Rick.

YOUR BELIEF WINDOW

"Before I was a coach, I had a long corporate career. In my thirties, I was an up-and-coming middle manager. I was all about delivering results, getting stuff done! In retrospect, my self-awareness was, let's just say, nascent. One day, our division head called me along with my boss and asked if I had a few minutes to meet with someone she had in her office. Hyrum Smith was at the time CEO of Franklin Planner (now Franklin Covey). Our company was a big customer. She explained he had a new

concept he developed. They wanted my opinion ⌣
be received with our managers if they included it in ⌣

"Smith took me through his idea, telling me that we all ⌐
a Belief Window through which we see the world," said Ric⌐
"He asked me to envision a small invisible windshield in front
of my face. On that windshield are beliefs. Some of them are
useful, but some are outdated. They used to help you, but now
they get in your way. They clutter up the windshield. They
block your vision. They warp your view. But, if you take the
time to evaluate them and get rid of the outdated ones that
no longer serve you, you'll have a clear picture in front of you.

"Well, later that day," said Rick, "I gave my feedback. I was dismis-
sive. I told them I thought it was daft and wouldn't fly with our
managers, who were too sophisticated for invisible windshields.
I returned to attacking my to-do list and getting things done.

"It took me a while," continued Rick, "and longer than I'd
like to admit, but finally it dawned on me that they didn't
want my *input*. My bosses knew it was something I needed to
hear. At that stage of my career, I thought it was *all* about the
results. Putting points on the board mattered most. I focused
much more on the *what* than the *how*. And my bosses knew
that would limit my effectiveness. I had blinders on and an
incorrect principle on my Belief Window. I needed to be more
balanced. Once I finally got it, I found it incredibly valuable.
And I've never forgotten it."

"We all carry around many deeply held beliefs that can dis-
tort our vision if they're left unexamined," said Rick. "This
is particularly true of people approaching retirement. Many

...dated beliefs on retirement we've internalized ...ving them a second thought."

...? what?" asked Pete.

"There are two I see most often," said Rick. "They're both about curiosity, or a lack thereof. And they can have harmful ramifications if left unchallenged."

TOO COOL FOR SCHOOL?

"The first one is embedded from an early age," said Rick. "Let me ask you, Pete, do you see yourself arriving in retirement as a finished product? Many people do."

"I see myself more as a work in progress," said Pete with a laugh.

"Well, I hear some people say they've learned everything they need to learn. Sometimes, they joke about it," said Rick. "But I'm not sure they appreciate how this belief can be self-limiting."

Rick's example of this ageist belief many people have is not the only common one. Others include:

- I am who I am. I'm not going to change now at my age.
- You can't teach an old dog new tricks.
- Retirement is the end of the line. It's all downhill from here.
- It is what it is.

We're quick to notice ageist beliefs in others. But without careful self-awareness, we can unwittingly harbor ageist assumptions ourselves. Some of those assumptions have been reinforced for decades. Many educational systems were built on the belief that learning was something you did early in life. You then went on to have a career, and maybe also raise a family. Then, you retired and relaxed for what was often a short time. There were three distinct phases of life, with the education portion frontloaded.[14]

Some people still believe their education phase of life ended with their formal schooling—many sincerely think they're too old to learn anything new. But a lot has changed. An increasing number of people today enter retirement knowing that life-long learning is possible and extremely valuable. Neuroscience research has proven this to be true. Researchers have discovered that the brain continues to create new neurons, pathways, and connections in adulthood through neuroplasticity.[15] It's a complex subject, but the headline is: you can still learn and grow if you're willing to work at it.

WHAT'S YOUR MINDSET?

"Some people aren't fully aware of their attitudes about how we learn," said Rick. "The educational system and the business world reinforce a certain mindset. But you can replace it with a better one—a growth mindset. And it will infuse your retirement with curiosity."

"Pete," asked Rick. "Are you curious about the growth mindset?"

"Sort of."

"Good," answered Rick. "Here's a short summary."

GROWTH VERSUS FIXED MINDSET

Research by Carol Dweck, a psychologist at Stanford University, pioneered a concept that has changed how education is approached. She found teachers and students had one of two mindsets that shape their approach to learning.[16] These two mindsets influence students' cognitive habits and how they perform in the classroom, especially when they encounter adversity. One perspective is limiting; one is empowering.[17]

The fixed mindset believes academic performance stems primarily from one's inherent ability. Results are attributed to endowed traits: "I got an A on the math test because I'm good at math." However, a student with a growth mindset would explain the same result differently: "I got an A in math because of the work I put in." The second student believes performance comes from learning through effort, embracing challenge, and resilience.

This difference can have profound effects over time. With a fixed mindset, criticism and failures are threatening to your self-image. You'll tend to stick to the familiar. You'll become less willing to experiment and take risks, which can eventually limit your learning. With a growth mindset, criticism becomes reframed as an opportunity to improve. Rather than responding defensively, you see critiques as opportunities to learn.

Have you ever worked with people who felt the need to show they're the smartest person in the room? With a fixed mindset, you continually need to prove yourself and establish the superiority of your innate abilities. A fixed mindset leads you to try to hide your weaknesses. In contrast, with a growth mindset, obstacles and shortcomings can be overcome with diligence and perseverance. Embracing challenges and focusing on your level of effort becomes your approach.

Rick asked Pete, "So, what do you think?"

"Well, it seems too black and white to me," answered Pete. "But I like knowing I can still learn and grow."

"I hear you," Rick replied. "The question is, Which way do you lean? And how far do you lean? In retirement, I'd lean hard in the direction of a growth mindset. It will keep curiosity in your life."

"Sounds good," said Pete. "But how do I get a growth mindset? What should I do, in practical terms?"

"Start with raising your awareness of how you react to failures and setbacks. Are you self-critical in those situations?" said Rick.

"I guess I tend to beat myself up then," replied Pete.

"Then let's reframe how you view criticism and failure. Step back, and rather than beating yourself up, ask yourself better questions. *What can I learn here? How can this help me become better?*" suggested Rick. "Tune in to your inner dialogue. Focus on what you can learn versus thinking of it in terms of your inherent traits."

IS RETIREMENT AN INSIDE JOB?

Pete's head was spinning. He had a lot to think about. As he was about to leave Rick's office, he noticed a well-worn copy of a book on his desk. "That looks interesting," Pete said.

"This? It's one of the most important books I've ever read. I keep it there to prompt me to re-read it every so often and remind myself that I can decide where to channel my attention."

The book was *The Inner Game of Tennis* by Timothy Gallwey, published in 1974. It isn't really about tennis. It's more about directing your attention to mute your inner critic. While teaching tennis just out of college, Gallwey had discovered that the harder he taught his students, the worse they played. Their play improved when he instead encouraged them to focus on an essential external variable, like the ball's spin as it crossed the net or the sound of the ball as it hit the court. He observed that shifting their focus tamped down their anxiety. It allowed them to learn and play more naturally. It brought out their best.[18]

PETE'S HOMEWORK

"Are you up for putting this into practice, Pete?" asked Rick.

"Sure," answered Pete, wondering what he was getting himself into.

"Good. Let's start small. Here's your homework."

"Homework?" Pete flinched.

"Calm down—all you have to do is complete these two work-sheets before we meet next. On the first, make note of the times when you feel bored. Jot down when it happens, how long it lasts, and how it feels. Simple. Don't overcomplicate it.

"On the second, create a running list of things you are curious about: things you'd like to learn more about, things you'd like to try."

When Pete arrived home that evening, he had a lot on his mind. He admitted to himself that he had become bored after he had been suddenly let go. It made him feel like he'd lost his mojo. Uncertainty had always made him anxious. Pete knew he was the type that liked to close all the loops. *Maybe there's something to this curiosity thing that can help me*, he thought.

The garage door broke his train of thought as Pete heard his wife Melissa coming home from work. Panic swept over him as he remembered it was his night to make dinner. Just as he was coming up with a plan on the fly, Melissa breezed in with takeout from his favorite restaurant. "Did you get my text? I thought you might be running late since you were meeting that coach today, so I picked this up. How did it go with Rick?" asked Melissa.

Pete gave her a quick summary, and asked, "How was your day?" It was a question he'd asked her countless times before, but this time it didn't feel like a perfunctory question. He was listening with sincere interest, asking follow-up questions wanting to know more.

After a while, Melissa interrupted him with a laugh. "What's up with the twenty questions? What's gotten into you?"

Sheepishly, Pete said, "I don't know. Just curious, I guess."

TAKEAWAYS

1. Boredom can be problematic in retirement if it's left unconfronted. Learn to be comfortable with some temporary boredom. But use it to your advantage and tune in to what it may be signaling. If you find yourself becoming bored longer term, dig down to identify what the root cause is and take action to address it.

2. Curiosity invigorates retirement. It can lead you to new interests, passions, and even a new purpose. Embrace the pursuit of lifelong learning. Become an investigator. Ask better questions and research subjects that interest and intrigue you. Engage your natural ability to learn new things. It can also enhance your relationships by making you a more interesting—and interested—partner, friend, or spouse.

3. Find out what's on your Belief Window. Some core beliefs don't change over the life course, but others become outdated and get in your way. You wouldn't run your iPhone using iOS 2.1. You'd do a software update. Don't fuel your retirement with beliefs acquired in your early life that no longer serve you. Update them.

4. Embrace a growth mindset. You can learn and grow at any age. You have the time now. Make the most of it and start learning.

5. Retirement encompasses your outer and internal selves, and that includes your inner dialogue. Turn down the volume on your inner critic by learning to challenge your thoughts and assumptions.

EXERCISE—YOUR BOREDOM & CURIOSITY AUDIT

1. When do you find yourself bored?
2. Which of these times are temporary and which are longer lasting?
3. What are you curious about learning more about or trying?
4. Which one are you most curious about?
5. What's one step you can take to find out more about it?

CHAPTER THREE

TAKE CONTROL OF CHANGE AND MOVE BEYOND THE STATUS QUO

"I only have three minutes, so I thought I'd give the secret to life. It's three words: Adapt, adjust, and revise. That's the advice I'd give my fifty-year-old self, and it's the advice that I followed myself. It's the way I adjusted to getting older..."[1]

—ALAN ALDA

Pete heeded Rick's advice on curiosity. He wrote out a long list of his interests, leading him to pick up the guitar again. Pete hadn't played since college. He was curious if he still had it. By the end of the week, he was obsessed with YouTube videos on guitar playing. One helped him relearn one of his favorite songs. *How did we get through college without the internet?* he wondered.

Playing again felt familiar, but it also felt brand new. Maybe he did still have it. Well, a little. Even his retired neighbor, Dave, noticed, remarking one day, "You sound much better, Pete. But will you be playing a new song anytime soon?"

Pete was realizing how much his life had changed. Being let go abruptly was a shock, but he had quickly fallen into a routine. It was quiet at home, lonely even. He was the only one at home during the day, except for Bailey, their black Lab, and she apparently shared Dave's opinion of Pete's repetitive riffs. She quickly left the room as soon as he picked up his guitar.

Pete was starting to appreciate the newfound flexibility he had. There was time to think. Some days, he felt he could get used to life at a slower pace. But he felt *off*. He wasn't used to not working.

One day, Dave asked him how he was doing. He explained what happened at Mega Corp. When Dave asked, "So, what's next for you?" Pete was surprised to answer, "I'm retiring early," with conviction.

A CHANGE FOR THE GOOD?

Driving to his next appointment with Rick, Pete thought about how he felt about the changes he was dealing with. He was struggling to find the right words.

As they caught up on what had happened since they last met, Rick was pleased to hear about Pete's renewed interest in the guitar. Pete told him about his conversation with Dave about retiring early.

"It surprised me to say it so convincingly. But I think it's because I've decided it is the right move for me," Pete said. "I know it's a big decision. Now I'm clear I'm retiring, but I'm still unclear about what comes next. I want to talk with you today about all the changes I'm going through. I guess the best word to describe how I feel is *adrift*.

"There's a lot I don't miss about work, but I do miss the people. Well, some of them, anyway. I was always in the loop. Now, it's rare to get a return text from my former colleagues. That's been a surprise. I guess I miss being a part of something important. On Saturday, we were at the farmer's market. Melissa introduced me to Bob, a new neighbor who's just moved in a few weeks ago. After we chatted for a while, he asked me what I do for a living. I hesitated, and Melissa jumped in and answered for me. She told Bob who I *used to be*. That got my attention."

Pete's experience is not unique. The loss of contact with former colleagues can be felt as a loss in social status. If the loss of social contact and status remain unaddressed, it can impair someone's adjustment to retirement and, eventually, their well-being.[2] The social consequences of retirement can be exacerbated in situations like Pete's, where factors beyond their control precipitated the decision to retire.[3]

But, like many things in life, it's ultimately less about what happens and more about how you respond. One study found people who retired abruptly were not any less happy than those who retired gradually. What mattered was the sense of control they felt over the transition to retirement.[4] Some people let change control them while others take control of change.[5]

Nonetheless, the loss of social connectivity hurts, and it can be harmful in the long term. Cultivating social support is a critical part of aging successfully.[6] But departing the workplace can be a blow to your self-esteem. You're going from being in the center of all the action to feeling invisible. But the good news is that after an initial hit, people's self-esteem tends to increase in retirement over time.[7] Another study of retirees found that finding new ways of *mattering*—making a difference to others—affects how well people adjust and how they feel emotionally in retirement.[8]

Pete was quiet for a moment and then asked, "Okay, how do I address these issues?"

Rick answered, "There are no quick answers. But we can work on these. Let's talk about what you'll have to overcome. We have a new opponent to grapple with."

SCOUTING REPORT: THE STATUS QUO

The human brain is a powerful processor of information, but our minds don't operate in isolation. Our emotions can cloud our thinking.

Humans crave shortcuts. They conserve energy and make the thinking process efficient. But shortcuts can twist our thought processes. In the early 1970s, psychologists Daniel Kahneman and Amos Tversky identified specific cognitive biases in rational decision-making. Their work spurred the creation of the field of behavioral economics.[9]

One of these cognitive biases is Status Quo Bias. It shows

up in various areas in life, such as making choices on investments and health practices. As humans, we prefer the current state and what's familiar. The Status Quo Bias is trying to protect us from making any change that we would perceive as a loss.[10] But what people really fear is regret. We want to avoid decisions we may live to regret, so we overvalue what's familiar.[11] We default to staying in our comfort zone. We play it safe. Doing nothing is always an option, and the Status Quo Bias often makes it an appealing option we're pulled toward.[12]

Status Quo Bias deludes us into thinking there's no reason to change. Why risk it? Everything is good just the way it is. The pull of the status quo is powerful. But stepping out of your comfort zone to get involved in new activities can help you grow.

Retirement is often not the only change people are dealing with. If you're retiring at any age, you're also getting older, and aging brings changes you'll need to adapt to. Some people view aging as being about inevitable decline. But it's not that simple or that negative. Psychologist Paul Baltes characterized aging as part of a life-long process of adapting, noting that every phase of life includes gains and losses.[13] Some declines are a fact of life. But there's a lot you can do to mitigate them, delay them, and age successfully.[14] One strategy is Compensation, in which you make up for what you can't do as well anymore by using different ways to accomplish the same goal or task.[15] You don't want the status quo to keep you away from things that can generate gains for you and be left with only the decline side of the equation.

TAKE CONTROL BY STARTING SMALL

"How do I defeat the Status Quo Bias?" Pete asked.

"By taking control," Rick said. "The big question is, What will your story be from here? What will your children be telling your grandchildren someday about your life and what you did next?"

Researchers underscore the importance of a sense of control in transition periods, where the rhythm of daily life is upended and your emotional state is thrown off. Some people experience ripple effects and become passive and disengaged, which can spark a downward spiral. When you're in a transition, it's essential to regain a sense of control.[16]

People who are retiring can regain control by moving away from the status quo and making small, positive changes to build new healthy habits. Starting small ratchets down the risk. You'll be less likely to fear regret because you're making a small investment.[17] It's easier to step outside of your comfort zone that way.

Structure is one of the losses people experience right away when they move away from full-time work. Work provided organization—now that's up to *you*. The flexibility to do what you want can be a blessing or a curse.

"How are you structuring your days now, Pete?" asked Rick.

"Things are pretty loose right now. There's not much structure other than taking care of our dog Bailey. That's become my primary responsibility."

"I'll give you an exercise to work through before we meet next. Let's try out a few things to add some structure around what's most important to you," said Rick.

"Sounds good," said Pete. "You mentioned habits. How do they relate to retirement?"

"We rely on our habits more than we realize. Around 40 percent of our behavior is habitual.[18] Our brains love rules of thumb. It makes things automatic and conserves energy when we don't need to think about things consciously. And that's what habits do. Habits matter. Research shows a significant portion of our subjective well-being, or happiness, comes from our habits."[19]

"But aren't new habits hard to create?" asked Pete.

"Yes, but there's a smart way," said Rick. He explained how BJ Fogg, PhD., Founder of the Behavioral Design Lab at Stanford University, created a way to take control of habits by *designing* them. Fogg's Tiny Habits Method helps you:

- Pinpoint the habits you want
- Design a tiny version to make it easy to start
- Anchor the habit to a behavior you consistently do already

And wire it in through positive emotion by immediately celebrating it.[20] "What's a new habit you'd like to add?"

"I'd like to get a good workout in early in the morning. That always gets me off to a good start. I'm out of shape after all that's happened. I haven't worked out consistently in weeks."

"No worries. We'll make progress gradually. First, we need to Design the habit. How do you like to exercise?"

"We have an exercise bike I like to ride."

Rick asked Pete to describe his usual morning activities.

"When I come downstairs, I always feed Bailey and take her for a walk."

"After you come back in, what's the very last specific thing you do?"

"I hang her leash up on the hook in our mudroom."

"Great. That's what we'll use as a Prompt. After you hang up Bailey's leash, I want you to ride the exercise bike. Start with five minutes."

"*Five minutes*? That's not going to get me back in shape," Pete said.

"We're starting *tiny*, remember," Rick said. "Technically, we should start with just getting on the exercise bike. We're working on getting the sequence down. Some habits grow naturally over time. You'll see.

"The third step is key. You are reinforcing it with positive emotion. So, take a look at this list of Celebrations. Which would you like to try?"

"Hmm. Some of these are interesting. How about I exclaim

YES! like the sportscaster Marv Albert used to say when he was announcing a basketball game?"

"Great. So, we have your recipe. This is your Tiny Habits Method statement: **After** I hang up Bailey's leash, **I will** ride the exercise bike and **celebrate** instantly with *YES!*"

Pete was skeptical that five minutes a day would help much. But he was willing to give it a try. It took time to get used to the Celebration, but it wasn't long before the sequence became automatic. Rick was right—within a few weeks, Pete was up to riding his exercise bike forty-five minutes a day. He was feeling much better already, and he was feeling confident he could change in other ways, too. Perhaps in some big ways.

TAKEAWAYS

Learn to accept and embrace change. Adapting to change is a crucial life skill, and it's vital in retirement. How well you adjust during the transition to retirement will significantly impact how satisfied you are in retirement.

Step out of your comfort zone. It's the pathway to ongoing personal growth. But the pull of the status quo is powerful. Fearing making decisions, you may regret what holds you back and prevents you from taking actions to lead to gains and growth.

Starting small reduces how you may perceive the risks of making changes. Change takes time. New techniques, especially the Tiny Habits Method, can kickstart your efforts and get you on track faster.

EXERCISE—BUILD A NEW HABIT

Ready to start small and design a new habit? Pick one new habit you'd like to create. Maybe it's walking more, eating less, working out, meditation, or reading more.

Use the Tiny Habits Method by BJ Fogg to start small. Use his three-step process to design your new habit.

After I _____ (do a behavior you already consistently do)

I Will _____ (the smallest tiniest version of your new habit)

And Celebrate by _____ (an immediate celebration, like a victory dance, or gesture)

Fogg recommends designing three new habits at a time. For more information, see his free five-day email course at tiny-habits.com, where you can design three new habits and get help from a Certified Tiny Habits coach online each day.

CHAPTER FOUR

ENHANCE SOCIAL CONNECTIVITY TO SIDESTEP LONELINESS

"Human beings are social creatures. We are social not just in the trivial sense that we like company, and not just in the obvious sense that we each depend on others. We are social in a more elemental way: simply to exist as a normal human being requires interaction with other people."[1]

—ATUL GAWANDE

Pete's multiple walks a day were helping him get back in shape, but he knew his new habit of getting on the exercise bike as soon as he came back from the morning walk was making the real difference. As he hung Bailey's leash and headed to the bike, Pete reflected on how automatic it had already become. He didn't have to psych himself up to do it—he just did it.

Both of these activities gave him time to think. But maybe too much time. Pete wasn't used to spending so much time alone.

RETIREMENT TAKES A VILLAGE

Humans are social animals. We're hardwired for relationships with others. We need friendship, companionship, and love. We yearn for a sense of belonging. We want to be a part of a community, something greater than ourselves. Ultimately, our close relationships with others give our lives meaning. Social connectivity plays a vital protective role in our health and well-being. Research indicates you'll have 50 percent less risk of early death with social connectedness and a reduced risk of depression, cognitive decline, and dementia.[2]

Multiple factors influence how someone's transition to retirement will unfold, but social connectivity is a key one. A socially connected retirement is an active and engaged one. It gets you *out and about* more. People with diverse social ties in retirement have higher physical activity levels and a less sedentary lifestyle.[3]

FINDING YOUR NEW TRIBE

Twice a year, Pete and Melissa met with Debbie, their certified financial planner, to review their finances. It was something Pete looked forward to. Debbie had earned their trust over the years. It was a good checkpoint on where they stood, but it was also an opportunity to talk about where they were heading. Debbie was highly skilled at asking just the right questions to help them pinpoint any adjustments they'd need to make.

As they walked down the street to Debbie's office, Pete's mind flashed back to their earlier meetings. Most were routine, but some stood out, like the day they set up 529 plans to save for their children's college education. It seemed like yesterday. But now, their daughter Anne was a sophomore, and their son Andy would be a freshman in the fall. Then there was the time when Debbie had advised them to max out their 401(k) contributions to fund their retirements. They had just bought their first home, and it was a stretch for them. They debated it for weeks. *I'm sure glad we listened. I feel like this meeting will be one of those pivotal ones,* Pete thought as they entered Debbie's reception area.

Debbie greeted them warmly. "I was so surprised to learn you decided to retire after what happened with Mega Corp."

Melissa quickly added, *"So was I."*

"With your decision to retire early, I've run an updated set of projections," Debbie said. "We'll talk through the assumptions, and we can discuss adjustments to the plan we may want to consider. The good news is that you'll be able to handle retirement financially, though there will be a few trade-offs. But first, bring me up to speed on your decision. How do you *feel?*"

"I'm feeling great! I'm working out every day. I'm enjoying the freedom and having time to think. It's great to have time to read again. I'm usually reading two at a time, one fiction and one non-fiction. That's been great."

Melissa chimed in, "And he's picked up the guitar again."

Pete asked Debbie, "What do you see in your clients who retire early? What's different about the ones who do well and those who don't do as well?"

"They all enjoy a honeymoon period at first. But the ones who thrive have moved on from their profession. They're not living in the past. They don't focus on what they retired from; they concentrate on what they're retiring *to*. They get involved with new things, they meet new people, and after a while, they're enjoying a new life on their own terms."

"New people?" asked Pete.

"Yes. The new activities naturally expand their social circles. And that's a real positive because retirement can be lonely, especially for some of my male clients. Some people struggle at first, particularly when so much of their social interaction came from work. When they stepped away, a lot of those relationships drifted away as well. That surprised them, especially how quickly it happened. I notice a little sadness with some of them. They seem isolated. I think they look back more than they look ahead."

"It has been a big change interacting much less with people than I did when I was working full-time," Pete admitted. "During the day now, most of my interaction is with Bailey, our black Lab. And I've become close with Alexa, too."

Melissa added, "I do think Pete's starting to feel a little lonely."

"Me? Nah, I have our neighbors. I have plenty of interaction."

Melissa didn't let that slide. "I wouldn't say you and our neighbors are even remotely close. And did you forget that Jason and Caroline just *moved*?"

Pete drifted off in thought for a moment. Jason and Caroline had moved into the neighborhood the same year they had, twenty-five years earlier. Their kids were the same ages and had walked to school together every day. Jason and Caroline had always been there. Now they were gone. He was happy for them with their move, but it made him feel sad as well.

Pete tried to change the subject. "Debbie, besides our financial plan, do you have any advice for me, based on what you've seen with your clients?"

Debbie thought for a moment. "Yes, three things. First, give yourself time to figure out what you want this new life to be. Don't jump in too quickly. Try different things before you make any commitments. Second, don't put off getting started too long either. Get involved with a few things that interest you. Try some new things. Do more with the ones that click, and drop the ones that don't. Finally, start to create a new social circle. You'll be fine once you find your new tribe."

"Debbie, Pete's started working with a retirement coach, which I think is helping him," added Melissa.

"Maybe we should all have lunch with my coach, Rick," suggested Pete. "It would bring together my entire Retirement Brain Trust."

"That would be great," Debbie said. "I look forward to it."

SCOUTING REPORT: LONELINESS

A week later, Pete was happy when Debbie and Rick hit it off at lunch. But, newly formed Brain Trust aside, Pete was starting to wonder if his otherwise shrinking social circle would derail his early retirement.

He decided to ask Rick to design one of his signature scouting reports around Debbie's thoughts about the importance of social connection.

"Social connections do provide a lot of benefits in retirement, but you have to work a bit to maintain them," Rick said, "Financial security is a strong predictor of overall health and longevity, but social connectedness predicts physical and mental health on average *four times* more strongly. And they're related, of course. Financial security gives you the time and resources to create and nurture social ties."[4]

"What we're up against is loneliness," said Rick. "It's become a significant problem. Just so we're clear, let's define loneliness."

"Loneliness is the subjective feeling that you're lacking the social connections you need."[5]

—VIVEK MURTHY, SURGEON GENERAL OF THE UNITED STATES

Studies show it's possible for people to feel lonely even when they're surrounded by other people. Loneliness is really about *connection*—or lack thereof.[6] People often incorrectly believe it's only an issue affecting older adults, when in fact:

- Loneliness is an emerging problem on college campuses.[7]
- It affects about a third of the population globally.[8]
- The UK has created a national strategy to address and combat loneliness in the UK.[9]
- The Surgeon General of the United States declared it an epidemic.

Loneliness is a serious threat to health and well-being, one that's greater than obesity.[10] Loneliness and weak social connections are associated with a reduction in lifespan similar to that caused by smoking fifteen cigarettes a day.[11]

The workplace is a highly social environment. There's plenty of interaction, and you develop many connections with people at work. When you undergo a major life transition, like retirement, all of that is disrupted. You go from being immersed in an active social system to suddenly being outside of it. And as you get older, you spend more time alone.

Sixty percent of Americans in their sixties are alone more than half of their day, seven hours a day alone on average versus 4.75 hours for people in their forties and fifties.[12]

—PEW RESEARCH CENTER

It's an adjustment. When you retire, your social ties change, and it can lead to shifts in your emotional well-being.[13] Losing the social structure work provides can be destabilizing emotionally. Those work relationships help provide a buffer against stress, and that buffer matters most in bad times.[14] People who don't have a broad network outside of work can quickly become lonely in retirement.[15] Research shows that loneliness tends to be higher among men.[16] And when people go through an involuntary retirement, that's been found to be associated with a higher level of loneliness.[17]

But it's not all bad news. Retirement can have a positive effect on your overall social connectivity over time. You have more time to cultivate social relationships than you did when you were working full time.[18]

While retirement disrupts some social relationships at first, research has shown that over time, the size of a retiree's social network stays about the same. Only the *mix* shifts significantly.[19] Retirement shuffles the deck of your network and social interactions. The share allocated to family increases, and the share allocated to work colleagues and friends decreases. Men tend to reduce interactions with colleagues more. Women tend to cull their friends and spend less time with less meaningful relationships.[20] As we get older, we become more selective about whom we spend time with.[21] People have a sense time is more precious and don't want to waste it. The percentage of time we spend with the family goes up, just like we saw in the pandemic.

Rick asked Debbie what surprised her most about her clients who retire. "I've been a bit alarmed by the number of divorces. I had read about 'gray divorce' becoming a trend, and I see it with some of my clients.[22] Sometimes, it's for the better. But other times, I see it hurting one or both of them. Those people seem lonely to me."

Rick piped in with a question: "Debbie, what's the number

one principle you use in constructing investment portfolios for your clients?"

"That's easy. Diversification," she responded.

"That's the foundation here, too," Rick said. "Just like our investments, our social networks are dynamic. Over time, some people drop from your circle, and you add others. It's like a portfolio of relationships, and it's wise to have a diverse one."

Studies confirm all relationships are not equally important. In general, stronger ties, like those with your family and close friends, are where you'll derive your greatest overall satisfaction in retirement. They're your inner circle. They'll also be your most intense relationships. But your inner circle of strong ties is only part of the story. We also have *weak ties*, and they matter, too. Weak ties are your more casual contacts, like acquaintances. Interestingly, research shows the number of weak ties someone has is a stronger predictor of positive aging and well-being than the number of strong ties. Weak ties are easier to maintain. They act as a kind of farm system. Research shows people with the greatest number of weak ties develop more close relationships over time, and some of those relationships eventually grow into strong ties.

What's often overlooked is that those weak ties—your outer circle of acquaintances—can be more valuable in specific ways. Our strong ties usually see the world the same way we do. They tend to draw information from the same places we do. Weak ties can offer different perspectives and be better sources of new information and ideas.[23] They're often helpful in making introductions to people we wouldn't otherwise meet.[24] And the right introductions can have a big impact. They can lead to the right part-time work or consulting opportunity, or maybe the right organization to get involved with as a volunteer or board member.

On the way home from lunch, Pete asked Melissa what she thought about the group's conversation. "I think Debbie's right," she said. "You need to find your new tribe."

Pete sighed, "I don't need a *tribe*. I'm lucky. I married my best friend." Melissa blushed, but Pete noticed she didn't say anything more.

Pete decided to break the silence and asked, "I'm your best friend too, right?"

Melissa looked away and then laughed, "Don't be silly. You're my husband. That's different."

A GAME PLAN

The next day, Pete and Rick met again. Pete got right to the point. "You've got my attention with loneliness. I'm concerned. What's the game plan?"

"Let's talk about how you could get started becoming more connected socially. Think small steps, as you did with building your exercise habit. Where could you begin to get involved that would bring new social interactions into your life? We're looking for things that interest you and could create shared experiences you'd find meaningful. That often involves helping others. Think about some interactions that would be of mutual benefit," said Rick.

Rick took Pete through a brainstorming exercise. They came up with several ideas on places where Pete could experiment with getting involved. There were a few local group activities and community programs he was interested in exploring. Perhaps he'd try volunteering. Taking a class also interested him, which led to a discussion of a course he could teach someday. But one idea appealed most to Pete: mentoring. It was something he enjoyed at work, and he had received positive feedback on his abilities over the years. Pete felt excited. There are some real possibilities here. *Maybe I won't become a hermit, after all,* he thought with a smile.

He was about to leave with his homework assignment to research these ideas when Rick asked him if anything else was on his mind.

"Actually, yes. I get the importance of social ties now. But maybe I should be concerned about my relationship with Melissa. That's the most important thing to me."

"What's going on?" asked Rick.

"We're coming up on our thirtieth anniversary in a few weeks. But I feel like Melissa and I are a little disconnected these days. She's consumed with her work. We don't spend time together like we used to. Maybe I'm not used to her being so busy, especially when I'm not. We were always *both* busy. It's different now. I can't wait until she comes home, but she's usually wiped out. And after dinner, she usually has work to catch up on. We're out of sync. I guess Debbie's tales of gray divorce have me a little paranoid.

"She is my best friend. And that's what's bugging me. I asked her if I am her best friend. Her answer was, 'You're my husband. That's different.' It shocked me a bit."

Rick explained this wasn't uncommon and cited some research.[25]

About two-thirds of husbands list their wives as their best friends.

But less than half of the wives list their husbands.[26]

Pete laughed. "Well, that makes me feel better. Sort of."

He paused as the research data sunk in. "As a matter of fact," said Pete, "this is reminding me of what's happening with Jason and Caroline, our neighbors who recently moved."

JASON AND CAROLINE'S STORY

Jason had his retirement meticulously mapped out. He was a brilliant software engineer, but he was different from many of his peers. He was outgoing and social. He thrived on interaction with people. He built a successful career at a Fortune 500 company and enjoyed his work—mostly. He loved problem-solving, but he disliked the politics that came with working for a large company. Over the years, he'd come to accept it as part of the job. But Jason had long had a dream for how he wanted to spend his retirement years. He wanted to retire early and had precisely mapped out his plan and investment strategy so he could do so at fifty-five.

He and wife Caroline shared a dream of moving to a warmer climate. Caroline took on the task of evaluating places they would consider moving to. She researched several states and multiple housing options. They had many discussions about the different choices. There was a healthy give-and-take, but they felt they were on the same page.

Refining the financial plan was right up Jason's alley. He made sure the numbers would work and also had a plan for his life after retirement. He had started on it when he first put his investment plan in place, twenty years before he retired.

Jason was a soccer player in college, a goalie. Not much got past Jason. While he loved designing software, his true love was coaching soccer, and he planned to do just that in his retirement. When his kids were young, he volunteered to coach in their local leagues. As they progressed, he became immersed in their competitive travel leagues.

As the youngest of their three children went off to college, so did Jason. His reputation as a youth soccer coach had caught the attention of the head coach of the women's team at a nearby college. There was only one problem: Jason was still five years away from retirement. But he worked things out with his boss to be able to do both. He shifted to working from home so he could attend practice at the end of his workday.

The part-time college coaching role was a perfect fit. The main focus of his role was recruiting talent. He was immersed in analyzing data on players, leveraging his connections with coaches in the region, and using his people skills to develop relationships with recruits and their families.

When he turned fifty-five, he and his wife were ready to move. Jason retired exactly as planned. They took a year to build a smaller place in a new Active Adults community in California. It gave them time to plan their transition. They were both excited about the move. Jason used his soccer network (including some of his weak ties) to find a new assistant coach role there.

He threw himself into his new coaching world in a different part of the country. It was an adjustment at first, but he quickly developed new relationships. The weather was great. Their new home was much smaller, yet somehow just right, with a spectacular view of the sixteenth hole of a new golf course and a sliver of the Pacific Ocean. The dream was now a reality. Except this time, something got past Jason, the former goalie. And it was a big miss.

It wasn't working for Caroline. The cross-country move was hard on her. She had grown up in the town they lived in, where she had deep roots with family and friends. When they moved, she had also retired from her job at the university. She missed the people she worked with there. Jason was off and running with soccer, and Caroline felt lonely without her friends and colleagues. Their new neighbors were nice, but she didn't feel like she had that much in common with most of them. The fifty-five-and-older community they'd moved to felt cliquey, and the activities didn't interest her much. She wasn't used to spending so much time alone. She felt like she was on an island. She was homesick. She wasn't herself. She wasn't happy. For the first time in their thirty years of marriage, she felt like she and Jason weren't in sync. Instead, she felt like they were drifting apart.

While they had meticulously researched their plan, they failed to recognize there were multiple social circles that needed to be rebuilt: the social circle they shared as a couple, Jason's social circle, and Caroline's circle. The last one was going to take some time and effort. Jason was beginning to wonder if they had done the right thing in moving. He was feeling guilty about his dream turning into a big mistake for them.

"Food for thought," said Rick. "It's worthwhile to test drive a new location so you know what it's *really* like to live there. Consider renting for a year before you decide to buy."

TAKEAWAYS

1. We're all social animals. The more socially connected you are in retirement, the more active and engaged you're likely to be versus becoming more sedentary and isolated. Social connectedness provides fun, joy, and protective health benefits.

2. Retirement disrupts the social ecosystem you're a part of at work. The emotional aspects of the transition demand your attention. When you retire, your social circle shifts more toward family and away from professional colleagues. The percentage of time you'll spend with family increases, as does the time you'll spend by yourself. Think about how you will replace the connectivity and interaction you have, or used to have, with work colleagues.

3. Don't sleep on your weak ties. They can be valuable connections and relationships you can cultivate.

4. Find your new tribe. There are many ways to build new social relationships in retirement, including volunteering, taking classes, and mentoring. Experiment with a few to see what works best for you. If you're still working, allocate some time to these activities in advance of retirement to make the transition smoother. If you have a spouse or partner, pay attention to all your social circles in retirement—the ones you share and your personal connections.

EXERCISE—YOUR SOCIAL CIRCLES

Moving on from the world of full-time work changes your social connectivity. It's wise to be prepared and open to building new connections. Let's take stock:

1. Approximately what percentage of your social activity is tied to your work?

2. What activities can you get involved with that may create new social connections?

3. List five weak ties that you'd like to tap into more. Think about friends of your friends, people who you know a bit and want to get to know more, and acquaintances who seem interesting.

4. How can you strengthen a few of those relationships?

5. How could those relationships help you?

CHAPTER FIVE

UNLEASH CREATIVITY TO VANQUISH INERTIA

"Retirement is a time to unlock dreams."[1]

—JULIA CAMERON

"Art class?" Melissa asked with raised eyebrows. "Seriously? Where's this coming from?"

"C'mon, I think it would be fun," Pete countered. "You do remember *fun*, right?"

"Very funny. You do remember that neither one of us has an artistic bone in our bodies," Melissa replied.

"That's okay. It's about trying something new," Pete said.

"All right. I'll give it a try if it's that important to you," Melissa said with a smile. "But you still haven't told me where this is coming from."

"It's my homework with Rick," Pete explained. "I'm research-ing the next scouting report. I'm thinking I should try doing something creative. Take a step outside my comfort zone."

"You got that part right. Okay, I'll add it to my calendar. I'm labeling it F-U-N—it better be."

SCOUTING REPORT: CREATIVITY AND INERTIA

Pete shared with Rick that he was feeling antsy to get out of limbo and get on with a new life. In his career, his sense of urgency had served him well. But he knew it was a double-edged sword. Rick reminded Pete to give himself time to get to the right place.

Pete was excited to share his contribution to the scouting report with Rick. He had prepared a detailed slide deck to summarize the key points. "I learned a lot," Pete said. "I decided to flip the script and scout the opponent last and the solution first. I know you always start with a definition. So, here goes."

Creativity is defined as the ability to produce work that is novel and useful.[2]

Creativity in older adults is a pretty new area of research. Over 72 percent of the studies on the topic have been done in the last twenty years.[3] A major one, *The Creativity and Aging Study*, was done by Gene Cohen at the George Washington University and illuminated the benefits people received from being involved with the arts.[4] Not only did their health improve, but they also had a higher level of social engagement. Cohen believed we have an "inner push," a drive for continued growth and creative expression that persists as we get older. In his view, retirement opens up a liberation phase, a time to experiment and explore more creative things.[5]

Being involved in artistic activities now and then is enjoyable but it doesn't do much else for you. However, *regular* engagement with the arts, and especially sustained involvement, is associated with enhanced well-being.[6] Serious, long-term engagement with various creative activities (such as music, art, dance, writing, pottery, sewing, or woodworking) is associated with higher life satisfaction.[7]

In her book on creativity in retirement, *It's Never Too Late to Begin Again*, Julia Cameron stresses that anyone can be creative. She notes we all have a well of creativity to tap with enough time and attention and the right tools. Echoing Cohen's research, she writes that while you may leave full-time work behind, "self-expression never stops."[8]

INERTIA

What gets in the way of creativity in older adults? The next opponent: inertia.

Here's a straightforward definition:

Inertia is a tendency to do nothing or to remain unchanged.[9]

For Pete, that definition struck a chord.

"That describes what it feels like when I stay in my comfort zone. It's the opposite of the picture Gene Cohen painted. Instead of an inner push nudging me to learn and grow, I find myself standing pat. There's no exploring, no experimenting, and no movement. I just get lost in Netflix," said Pete.

Rick interjected, "Okay. But explain to me what you've discovered about how inertia *works*."

"It reminds me of our first opponent, boredom," said Pete. "They're related, but different. Boredom lulls you, but inertia dulls you. It's heavier, like a weight. It hits the pause button on your inner drive. It's like living life with the emergency brake on. You can't get going. Boredom is more temporary. Inertia sets in for the long haul. You get used to it. It becomes comfortable. It gets progressively harder to step out of it and get moving. It's like when you stop working out for a while. You get used to that. Every day that goes by, it's harder to start back up again. After a while, the idea of working out feels like climbing a huge mountain."

Pete continued, "You get in the habit of seeing things the same way. You avoid thinking things through from a different perspective. I remember one of my bosses confiding in me once that he thought one of my colleagues was mentally lazy. He noticed he wasn't willing to invest the energy to look at something from multiple angles. I resolved then to never have that said about me."

"So, inertia gets in the way of thinking differently?"

"Exactly. By staying in our lane, we're locked into our perspective. It can be narrow and limiting. We're less likely to come up with a unique idea or combination of ideas."

"But it goes beyond that," Pete said. "Inertia leads you to believe that there's minimal upside in trying to continue to learn and grow."

"Why's that?" asked Rick.

"It's easier to stick with what you know. There's comfort in the tried and true. There's a risk in venturing out to try new things. There's no guarantee it will work."

"And you might look foolish," Rick added.

Pete laughed. "Yes, but I can assure you that's not a big deal. I know exactly what that feels like. I did my homework. I joined an art class."

STEPPING OUT OF THE COMFORT ZONE

It was pouring rain as Pete and Melissa hustled from their car to enter the Arts Council building. Despite Melissa's reminder, Pete had left the huge golf umbrella in the garage. Now they were soaked through. "It's fun so far," she said through a forced grin.

They were greeted by a smiling woman offering two towels. "Hi, I'm Terry. Welcome. Let me introduce you to others in the class. We'll be getting started in a few minutes."

They entered a bright room with ten people of various ages in a semicircle of easels. The smell of paint hit Pete right away. It transported him back to the third grade. He loved the art class then. But now, here they were at Introduction to Watercolors for Beginners.

"Away we go," said Melissa.

Terry's introductory remarks to the class seemed to set everyone at ease. "Over the next twelve weeks, we're here to learn together and support each other," she said. "Permit yourself to use your imagination and experiment. But most of all, get to know each other and have fun."

She then emphasized the concept of the Beginner's Mind from Zen Buddhism. "Leave your preconceived notions at the door and bring an open mind to this experience," she explained. "And consider yourselves warned: this class is about more than painting. It's about changing how you see and how you think."

Each student took a few minutes to introduce themselves. Pete could tell everyone was eager to learn. He noticed several people mentioned they were returning to something they loved to do when they were much younger.

It took a while for Pete and Melissa to get going. But toward the end of the class, Pete was genuinely having fun. So was Melissa. While her work showed more attention to detail, Pete's was more abstract. But they both were enjoying it. Pete even laughed it off when one of their classmates complimented his initial work. "Hey, that's a great start. What's your cat's name?"

"Our dog's name is Bailey," Melissa said, trying hard to contain her laughter.

Melissa was upbeat as they drove home. "I have to admit it *was* fun. I like Terry and the people in the class. I'm glad we're doing this together."

SCOUTING REPORT PART TWO: DIVERGENT THINKING IN DAILY LIFE

Rick picked up where they left off at their next session and began his part of the scouting report. "I'm glad you brought up boredom from the earlier rounds. As things progress in the Retirement Game, you'll start to see connection points with earlier opponents. For example, it turns out that boredom can be a catalyst for creativity because the experience of being bored alerts us to seek out a variety or a new challenge.[10] The silver lining in these opponents is they can bring out the best in you by pushing you to change."

Creativity is not just about art. Gene Cohen's work went beyond the arts. Cohen wrote about "Big C" creativity, which includes great works of art, and "little c" creativity, which is how we innovate in daily life.[11]

Creativity in other areas of life starts with how we think. Divergent thinking is about being able to put things together in novel ways. It's thinking outside the box. Divergent thinking is enormously helpful when you apply it to daily living. It helps you apply the practical wisdom you've earned over your lifetime. From experience, we all have a deep reservoir of observations that helps us recognize patterns. We can come up with solutions that aren't as apparent to others who don't have the same accumulated experience. A great example comes from Gene Cohen's obituary. His in-laws had taken the train to Washington, DC, to spend the holidays with Gene and his wife. When they arrived at Union Station, a blizzard was underway, and Gene couldn't get into the city to pick them up. They couldn't find a taxi anywhere. But Gene's father-in-law had an idea. He found a pizza place nearby that was open and delivered. He ordered a pizza to be delivered to Gene's place in the suburbs and asked if he and his wife could come along for the ride.[12]

A CREATIVE RETIREMENT

Creativity can also be applied to planning for retirement. People are inventing their own custom approach rather than following the examples of their friends, neighbors, or parents. They start by getting clear about what they care most about. Creativity then helps them come up with alternative ways to achieve that vision. How people think about the transition period can encourage or suppress creativity. Taking an original approach can facilitate a better adjustment to retirement. Ryan Fehr, a University of Washington professor, challenges the assumption that the transition to retirement is always stressful. He argues that for some people, the freedom it offers leads to a refreshing and rewarding phase.[13] In his view, retirement can be a self-actualizing event. He notes that people with more creative personalities are used to seeking novel experiences. They're used to embracing new challenges. Retirement becomes just another role transition that their previous experiences have prepared them to approach with an open mind.[14]

Even those who don't consider themselves creative discover it's never too late to enhance their creativity. Author Tony Schwartz shared his experience taking a drawing class after years of working as a journalist. He firmly believed creativity was a genetic gift some people possessed and was convinced he wasn't one of them. But, in a five-day drawing workshop, he learned this belief was a self-created obstacle. His professional life had reinforced it. Day by day, his job had strengthened the use of his left brain. The workshop taught him how he could be creative by tapping into his whole brain.[15]

More people today are taking a creative approach to retirement by thinking about the role of work differently. A traditional retirement eschews work. The whole point is to leave it behind. But more people today are finding ways to continue working in a way that suits them. Working in retirement may sound like an oxymoron, but for some people, keeping work in the mix provides purpose, meaning, and challenge. While a traditional retirement takes an all-or-nothing approach, a creative retirement explores flexible options for people who aren't entirely *done* yet. Alternatives such as bridge jobs, part-time work, and consulting open up avenues to craft a version of semi-retirement that suits them well. And following a corporate career, some people choose to reinvent themselves as entrepreneurs.

Like Lee Weinstein, for example.

PROFILE

Lee Weinstein was fifteen years into his career in public relations at Nike when he began feeling like he wasn't learning anymore. It was the impetus for a period of introspection and reflection on what he wanted to do next. Before he decided to start his PR firm, which he runs today, he worked with a career coach. She advised him to take a break from going 180 kilometers an hour down the Autobahn and challenge his brain differently. She told him, "Go throw pots, go paint pictures." Lee took her advice.

Ultimately, Lee started a process with his wife Melinda of imagining their future year by year, working with butcher block paper. Posting photos of their Life Plan on Facebook led to suggestions that he share this process with others. One thing led to another, and he and his wife created a series of Life Planning workshops, which spawned a book on Intentional Life Planning: *Write. Open. Act.*

Lee shared how early experiences can stunt our thinking about what's possible. He said, "I think a lot of us have a lot of old scripts based on things that we've been told. Somebody told you at some point, 'You can't draw.' And then we sort of believe, 'I can't draw.' So, I think there's a lot of that stuff that we get told that can prohibit us.

"I think we also have to permit ourselves to know that we're just beginners. I remember I started doing some painting, and I was painting by the side of our road, and our neighbors drove by our road. They're like, 'What are you doing there?' And our kid, who's an art teacher, said, 'You know, Dad, that was pretty good, what you did.' Sometimes we need some good feedback. Sometimes we need some reaffirmation, but sometimes we need some coaching. We need to go take a class. Sometimes we just need to go do something weird."

AN UNEXPECTED CREATIVE OUTLET

Pete was looking forward to his next art class. Rick had also stoked his interest in how he could use creativity in his daily life. He hadn't come up with any practical ideas yet, but his wheels were starting to turn.

At the moment, though, Pete was waiting in the reception area of the local SCORE office downtown. SCORE is a resource affiliated with the Small Business Administration that provides free business mentoring to entrepreneurs.

Pete had been thrilled to get an unexpected call from Jim, a former boss. It was great to catch up. It felt like old times. And just like back in the day, Jim had called him for a reason—he needed Pete's help. Since retiring ten years earlier, Jim had volunteered as a mentor with SCORE. He loved helping small business owners with guidance, mostly on starting a business.

Jim called Pete because he said he'd caught a unique fish this time. Matt was younger than others he had mentored, and he was much more innovative. He had a business idea that looked promising. Jim thought it could be big, but Jim sensed he wasn't helping Matt much. Matt needed someone with a different point of view, someone who could challenge and expand his thinking. That's why he called Pete.

Matt was an engineer who had developed a prototype of a new technological device in the music industry. He was seeking investors to access capital to fund the launch. His idea was complicated, but it stood out so much that he landed a spot on *Shark Tank*. While it was an exciting experience, Matt was shot down. Weeks later, he was still reeling from the stinging critiques he'd received from Mr. Wonderful, Kevin O'Leary.

But while he departed disappointed, he left with valuable insights. Now, he was trying to figure out how to operationalize those ideas. But he was stuck. Pete agreed to meet Matt for a brainstorming session at SCORE. After two hours, Pete left exhausted. Jim told him how brilliant Matt was, but he hadn't warned him how difficult Matt was to work with. He was argumentative, closed-minded, stubborn, opinionated, and obstinate. And those were just the nice things Pete had to say.

But Pete left feeling he had helped Matt start to move forward. Toward the end, Pete noticed Matt listening more, resisting less, and showing more openness to some of Pete's suggestions. Matt even decided to change a key part of his pitch deck based on Pete's recommendation.

The hard-won victory of making an impact on Matt made Pete realize he might have a knack for this. Maybe mentoring would be a way for him to tap into his creativity in his new life. Being open-minded had helped Pete once again see how retirement could be full of new opportunities.

TAKEAWAYS

1. Staying in your comfort zone is tempting. It's familiar and feels safe. But staying in it too long is limiting and constricting. Tune in to your Inner Push for continued growth to break free of inertia.

2. Exploring art can have multiple benefits, including intellectual stimulation, social interaction, and improved health

and well-being. Retirement offers the time to experiment with different types of art. Explore, try, and ultimately pursue one or more types that spark your interest.

3. Everyone can be creative. You may have been told you're not a creative or artistic person, but with time, support, and sustained engagement, you can access your creativity. Embrace a Beginner's Mind to cultivate yours.

4. Creativity takes many forms. Beyond art, being creative in your daily life offers practical benefits. Find ways to apply the wisdom from your life experience to develop novel solutions to challenges and problems. Be open to unexpected opportunities to be creative and think differently.

5. A creative retirement looks past the traditional pathways others have followed and shines a light on an alternative way that's right for you. Consider different ways to meet your unique needs and priorities. Take control of retirement to shape it around your core values and what's calling you at this stage of life.

Whether you consider yourself a creative person or not, let's take a few minutes to explore your creative side:

EXERCISE—CREATIVITY

1. What artistic or creative things did you like before you began your working life?
2. What artistic or creative endeavors interest you now?
3. On a scale of one to ten (one = low, ten = high), how much out of your comfort zone are each of those?
4. What's your first step to get involved?
5. What's one area in your daily life where you could apply creativity?

CHAPTER SIX

EMBRACE ACCEPTANCE TO MANAGE EXPECTATIONS

"Frustration always results from a discrepancy between your expectations and reality."[1]

—DAVID BURNS

The morning walk with Bailey was taking longer today. Pete had a lot on his mind. He was lost in thought about his future. He was also noodling ideas to help Matt from SCORE on his product launch. He was looking forward to his coaching session with Rick this morning. There was a lot to talk about.

FRUSTRATION REIGNS

Rick opened up Pete's next coaching session with his customary question, "What would be the most helpful thing for us to focus on today?"

Pete was sullen. "Maybe I was naïve. I thought I'd be off and running in my next life by now. But I'm not, and it's driving me crazy," he said. "It's frustrating."

"When you're frustrated, it's wise to look at your expectations," said Rick. "More often than not, when you examine them, you'll find they're unreasonable, unrealistic, or irrational. Taking the time to really think about your expectations around retirement will help you get out of limbo."

SCOUTING REPORT: EXPECTATIONS

Expectations can be powerful influences. In a 2021 survey, over 75 percent of retirees with an average time in retirement of eight years said their life in retirement falls short of their expectations.[2] Our brains are predictive machines. We crave certainty about what the future may hold. We create forecasts of what we want to happen and what we think may happen. Problems arise when expectations take on a life of their own and are left unexamined and untested.

Expectations come from multiple sources. Sometimes, we're not fully aware of them. Furthermore, they're not always accurate. Many expectations come from social norms and the way something *should* be. People often give weight to the expectations of others, especially those people who are important to us. We want to live up to what we perceive those expectations are. Finally, we have expectations for ourselves. They can be strong motivators or sources of stress if they're not reasonable. But frustration is helpful if we use it as a signal for change, and that usually means it's time for reality-testing our expectations and perhaps recalibrating them.

That was a sticking point for Pete. He was reluctant to adjust his expectations.

"It sounds like you're saying I should lower my standards. I don't like that. I want to keep the bar high. My philosophy is if I fall short, I'm still likely to be way ahead," said Pete.

"In your business career, that may have been helpful to you. But there's a price to pay if you're setting expectations too high. It's stressful. Now that you've taken early retirement, it's wise to set the bar lower for yourself, at least in some areas of your life."

"Maybe," sighed Pete, "but having high standards is who I've always been."

"Let's talk about what's best for who you want to be *now*," Rick said. "Remember, you've never been thrust into early retirement before."

DO YOU EXPECT LIFE TO FOLLOW A PREDICTABLE COURSE?

Transitions take time. When we think about the overall direction of our lives, our expectations may be unrealistic, and they can leave us unprepared for the challenges that inevitably arise. Bruce Feiler, author of *Life Is in the Transitions: Mastering Change at Any Age*, interviewed 225 people from all walks of life about their life stories. His analysis of their experiences revealed that people tend to expect life to unfold in a predictable, linear fashion with common milestones at different ages. Yet Feiler found the life stories he heard were consistently *non-linear*. The average person in his Life Story

Project encountered a disruptive event every twelve to eighteen months. He also discovered that people face a significant transition point, which he dubbed a "Lifequake," between three to five times in their lives.[3] Feiler's data also indicates it takes some time to work through a transition. It's not usually a quick pivot—quite the opposite.

EXPECTATIONS OF RETIREMENT LIFE

Societal expectations of retirement sway us. People have views on what retired people should do and what they should not do. There's a set of norms and milestones we've internalized about retirement. Although those norms are becoming outdated, they persist. When someone has a different vision and timetable for their retirement, they can get a lot of pushback from other people. Many preconceived notions about retirement are negative and ageist. Research indicates such stereotypes about retirement can carry weight. They can affect how we think about retirement; they can also influence health outcomes and longevity.[4] But some stereotypes are positive.

In a study of over 1,000 people over twenty-three years, participants who espoused positive stereotypes about mental and physical health during retirement lived longer than negative thinkers, 2.5 and 4.5 years, respectively.[5]

Family members and coworkers have views about your retirement plans. How optimistic or pessimistic they are about their own retirement can color their opinions about your retirement plans. The opinions of others can shape your thinking and have a significant effect when people do not pre-plan how they'll invest their time in retirement.[6] It's good to get input from others, but without developing a clear vision of your retirement, others can have undue influence. That may not be in your best interest, even when others are well-intentioned.

ARE YOU STILL KEEPING UP WITH THE JONESES?

Expectations, as an opponent, don't go it alone. It enlists our neighbors, friends, and co-workers to tempt us to play *Keep Up with the Joneses*. As human beings, we're very conscious of our social standing. It's a fundamental motivation. It boosts our self-esteem. Research has shown many people care more about status than they do about money. We're continually engaged in social comparison of how we're doing relative to others. Retiring involuntarily can shake up your sense of status. When something threatens our social status, it creates anxiety.[7] It stirs up negative emotions. One study demonstrated that people who compared themselves frequently to others experienced more guilt, regret, and blame than participants who engaged in less social comparison.[8] Such comparisons can even harm our physical health as they have a significant influence on how we perceive our well-being.[9]

Trying to keep up with the Joneses is a fool's errand. People often find out that the Joneses are overextended financially to keep up appearances. However, that doesn't stop us from thinking we should be living the same lives they are.

This is another way expectations deceive us—by creating a false sense of obligation. Psychologist Albert Ellis, who created Rational Emotive Therapy, colorfully encouraged people to stop "shoulding" on themselves.[10] In his view, telling yourself that you should be doing something—or not doing something—leads to irrational expectations. For example, having expectations about where we *should* be at various milestones in life can lead to behaviors driven by fear or anxiety more than by rational choice.[11]

HOW TO DEFEAT EXPECTATIONS

"I get it. Forget the Joneses. For some people, it's more about the show than the dough. It sounds like expectations is another opponent that distracts you by manipulating your thinking," Pete said.

"Exactly," confirmed Rick. "You may remember in one of our early matches where we learned about cognitive distortions. Expectations bend your perception of what is really happening. You end up concentrating on exaggerated things rather than on what's really at play. It's like a head fake. It gets you leaning in one direction instead of staying centered. In basketball, players are taught to stay focused on their opponent's torso because when that moves, that's what you want to follow. That way, you don't fall for the fakes."

"So, what's the game plan to beat expectations?" asked Pete.

ACCEPTANCE

Expectations lure us into focusing on how we think things should ideally be. Having a more objective, grounded picture of reality helps us make better decisions. The following three-step approach can help:

CLARIFY EXPECTATIONS

Expectations are often unstated or assumed. In that way, expectations can create ambiguity. The first play is to clarify what other people's expectations are and communicate what yours are of them.

Stew Friedman, an organizational psychologist at the Wharton School, created a process to clarify key people's expectations in our lives.[12] Freidman found that our *perception* of what people expect from us frequently exceeds what they *actually* expect. He recommends having structured conversations with your key relationships, at work and in life, about what they expect from you—and what you expect from them. Listening carefully and getting concrete leads to a clear understanding of expectations.

People who complete this exercise often report feeling relieved, as they thought others expected much more from them. They were also surprised by things that mattered more to people than they realized. Some of those things simply weren't high on their radar, but they were relatively easy to address once they learned how important they were to the other person. When you get on the same page and remove ambiguity, unrealistic expectations lose their power. When there's clarity, there are fewer misunderstandings.

ACCEPT REALITY MINDFULLY

The second step is to be more mindful. When you reflect on your expectations, you quickly realize they're future-focused. Therefore, by definition, they are imagined, not real. There's value in paying more attention to what is real: the present.

Ellen Langer has written extensively about mindfulness. In her view, mindfulness is a state of active engagement, in contrast to *mindlessness*, which is passive and limiting:

> *"Mindfulness is a strategy to lessen self-evaluation and heighten attention on the present."*[13]
>
> —ELLEN LANGER

When you operate in a mindless mode, you're on autopilot. And you get locked into one narrow mindset. It limits your ability to notice things. It creates blinders, and you miss what's going on around you.

In a mindful state, you're more attentive to what's happening in the present. You're better able to notice subtle cues and nuances. You are more likely to be able to evolve your views in light of new information.

When you create an Expectation, you tend to look at things only through that lens. It's highly subjective, and it biases your thinking. You're evaluating things against the Expectation and ask, *Am I falling short?* But that may not be the whole story.

If you're mindful, however, you can plug into reality, what's really happening. That helps you make adjustments, including revising your expectations.

ACCEPT YOURSELF

"The third step is perhaps the most important—learn to accept yourself," said Rick.

Self-acceptance is about having a positive attitude about yourself that's rooted in who you are, not in the external markers of success.[14]

Human beings are good at deception—we can even delude *ourselves*. Before you enter retirement, you may have come to define yourself by your professional titles, your achievements, and your status. Yet, you're much more than those things. When they fade as you retire, it can be disorienting. Psychologists Shelley Carson and Ellen Langer write that taking an honest look at our *authentic* selves is a vital step toward taking ownership of our future. They recommend accepting ourselves as a work in progress and remembering to use humor versus self-criticism.[15]

Healthy eating and getting enough sleep and exercise are important building blocks for a long, healthy life. But it's not just the body people need to take care of—the mind matters, too. A study of over 7,600 people over twenty years found that self-acceptance and helping other people were associated with decreased mortality risk.[16]

THREE STEPS FOR PETE

"Have you and Melissa talked through your expectations for retirement? Both yours *and* hers?" Rick asked.

"Not specifically, no. She's been very busy with work. I'm not worried about that, though. We're usually on the same page," answered Pete.

"Okay. But if I asked you to share with me what Melissa's hopes and concerns are for *her* retirement, what would you say?"

"Well," Pete hesitated. "I would say, 'Can I get back to you on that?'"

"It's worth having a good conversation about it," Rick advised. "It's a topic many couples avoid."

A survey asked couples separately when their spouse was planning to retire.

Fifty-seven percent got it wrong.[17]

"In light of all this, what action steps do you want to commit to taking and by when?" Rick asked.

"There are three things I'll do. First, I want to talk with Melissa about her expectations for her retirement and *our* retirement years," replied Pete.

"But before I have that discussion with Melissa, I want to have that conversation you recommended about what she expects from me. With how much our lives have changed this year, maybe I'm not in sync.

"Third, I want to clarify my expectations about creating my new life in early retirement. Maybe I'm too eager to move forward."

Before he left, Pete had a gift for Rick. It was a self-portrait he'd made in art class. The instructor had asked the class to paint something they had a strong emotional connection to. The painting depicted Pete suspended in mid-air. He had titled it *Limbo*.

"I'm struck by the expression on your face in the painting. What were you trying to convey?" Rick asked.

"Hope," said Pete. "I despise being in limbo, but I do have high expectations for my future."

TAKEAWAYS

1. Expectations can carry more weight than they should if they're unexamined. Reflect on your expectations for retirement. What are they based on? How are they shaped by cultural notions of retirement that may no longer be relevant? Examine and challenge your assumptions. Identify unreasonable expectations (like "*shoulds*") that you want to let go of.

2. *Keeping Up with the Joneses* is a distraction. Is it time to let that go?

3. Clarity and alignment take time to build. If you have a spouse or significant other, open a conversation about your hopes and concerns for retirement. Talk about where you each see yourself living as a couple and what you'd ideally like to be doing. Avoid critiques and judgment. Just share

your initial thoughts. Ensure you enter the conversation in a true listening mode with an open mind. Let your spouse and significant other talk first. Really listen. Look for where you're aligned and explore the places where you have different views. Expect this to be a series of conversations and give them the proper space and attention that the topic of your future together merits.

EXERCISE—KEEPING IT REAL WITH EXPECTATIONS

Forget the Joneses. Keep up with Pete by having conversations with key people in your life on expectations and with retirees to calibrate your expectations of what life in retirement is really like. Extra credit: start a mindfulness practice. There are books in the Resources section that can help you.

1. Initiate conversations with the key people in your life about what they expect of you and what you expect from them. You may be surprised at the outcomes.
2. Talk with people in various stages of retirement to get a realistic picture of their experience. How does that shift your expectations?
3. Begin a mindfulness practice to strengthen your ability to be attentive to the present moment, broaden your perspective on reality, and enhance your self-acceptance.

CHAPTER SEVEN

BOOST SELF-EFFICACY TO DEFEAT UNCERTAINTY

"In order to succeed, people need a sense of self-efficacy, to struggle together with resilience to meet the inevitable obstacles and inequities of life."[1]

—ALBERT BANDURA

At their next meeting, Pete caught Rick up on his progress with expectations.

"Melissa and I have started to talk, which is good. But I've realized this will take longer than I anticipated. We're going away for a long weekend in the Catskills, and we've agreed to talk then. It's a three-hour drive, and we'll be doing a lot of hiking, so we'll have lots of opportunities. I can't remember the last time we were away, just the two of us, without the kids or Bailey.

"I also did some soul-searching about what I expect of myself.

I know I'm expecting too much, too fast. I thought I'd find that one thing that would consume me as much as my job did—a new mountain to climb. But now I realize I want to do a variety of things, not just one big thing.

"And I've taken up your suggestion on mindfulness. I've started to meditate three days a week, using an app. I started small, and I'm only doing five minutes of meditation at this point. But I intend to keep building it up gradually. I do feel different on the days when I do it, more relaxed and focused."

"Sounds like you're ready to take on another opponent," Rick said.

Scouting Report: Uncertainty. The next challenge many retirees face is uncertainty. Uncertainty creates doubt, mistrust, suspicion, and a lack of conviction. It thrives when circumstances are less predictable. Almost two-thirds of Americans report that uncertainty about the future is a source of stress.[2] It's everywhere you turn when you're transitioning to retirement. It amplifies your emotions and feeds anxiety, which can lead to a host of problems.[3]

Uncertainty is the absence of clarity.[4]

Anxiety about the future can be exhausting. When you get caught up in worrying about what *might* happen, it takes you away from doing things to move forward. You're unsure of which way to go. You don't want to make a mistake. You feel like you're in a hall of mirrors. Different people tend to react differently to uncertainty. For those who are more sensitive to it, uncertainty can be paralyzing.[5]

Such was the case for Pete.

As part of the previous session's homework, Rick had provided Pete with a questionnaire called the Intolerance of Uncertainty Scale.

According to Pete's results, he had a high intolerance for uncertainty. He was the type of person who's thrown for a loop by uncertainty. He craved clarity, and when he didn't have it, he tried to manufacture it. He was an overthinker and a planner, the type of people most affected by uncertainty.[6]

Planners spend a lot of time and energy anticipating scenarios, which is even tougher to do when things aren't clear. There's almost an endless number of things that *could* happen once you start thinking about it. Trying to predict the future is a way some people attempt to regain some sense of control, but ultimately, they're just spinning their wheels.

Another way people try to cope with uncertainty is by ignoring it. It's their attempt to get distance from their problems and avoid dealing with how they're feeling emotionally. And while avoidance may seem like it protects you from the issue, it is a big drain on your energy.[7]

There are practical approaches to reduce uncertainty. Try to pay attention to when you're conjuring up all the things that *could* happen. Then, work with a way to narrow down the problem that fits the particular situation you're dealing with.

For example, rather than dealing with a big issue like retirement, which can be overwhelming, break it down into smaller, more manageable parts. Focus on what you can control rather than obsessing about what you can't.

Learning new skills also helps with uncertainty. Learning something new involves taking risks, but you're taking steps to build your capabilities. It helps you gain a sense of control. And finally, accept that uncertainty is an inherent part of this phase of life. You have to get comfortable with that and learn how to manage it.

When you embrace uncertainty as a normal part of later life, it can broaden the range of tools you use to plan for retirement. Plan financially for retirement in an analytical and quantitative manner. Crunch the numbers, but also envision what your life will be like. This type of preparation is more qualitative and non-linear and less about detailed planning and more about thinking it through. It requires more imagination.[8] In this part of planning, you're writing a story, the story of your future. Brian David Johnson, Intel's first futurist, notes, "One of the most underutilized tools in financial planning is your imagination, because you've got to imagine what you want your future to look like. And then, once you can imagine it, then you can start to achieve it."[9]

Bring your whole brain to planning for retirement. The details matter, but so does imagination.

SCOUTING REPORT PART TWO: SELF-EFFICACY

The late Albert Bandura is one of the most cited psychologists of all time, and he developed the Self-Efficacy Theory back in the 1970s.[10] His research-based model emphasizes the importance of believing you have the capabilities to influence the direction of your life.

You're the primary agent of change in your life. You have the personal agency to design your signature version of retirement.

Bandura argues that while people face different circumstances in life, we're not bystanders. We're not just a passive product of our circumstances. He found that people can gain more control and sway outcomes if they believe their choices and behaviors matter.[11] Recognizing that you have personal agency means you understand that what you do *matters*. Think of it as taking charge of your future because you know you can impact how things turn out. Accepting agency is not a trait some people are born with and others are not—it's something anyone can do at various stages across the lifespan.[12]

Uncertainty can impact your thoughts on agency because if you don't believe you can change things, you are less likely to invest the energy and effort to try.

Research has found that those who felt they had more control of their transition to retirement had *less* anxiety and more positive outcomes in their life in retirement.[13] While self-efficacy gives you the sense you can influence the course of events, cultivating optimism reinforces the belief that you're likely to succeed in doing so.[14] It sounds simple, but it matters. Bandura points out that people will only step up and deal with a challenging transition if they expect they'll be successful.[15] It's the foundation of resilience. Without self-efficacy, people will focus more on the threats than framing them as challenges. They're more likely to give up too soon or shy away from grappling with the tough issues in the first place.

"I think that's why some people withdraw when they first retire," said Rick. "The life they knew is over, and they don't think they have what it takes to build a new one. They resign themselves to the cards they've been dealt. They feel sidelined, and some people stay on the sidelines."

Research shows that the most successful people tend to get stuck the most, at first. They tend to think of themselves and their jobs as synonymous. When the job is no longer there, it's disorienting. They feel the loss of status most profoundly.[16] Studies have found that people who tied their identities closely to their work are more likely to encounter a decline in their mental well-being when they begin retirement.[17] Those retiring who had the most consistent upward trajectory in their careers have the most difficulty adjusting to retirement.[18]

"Well, I'm very confident in my ability to influence things," said Pete.

"Okay," said Rick, "I believe that. But that was you at *work*. What about now? How do you feel about your ability to influence your future?"

"I believe I can take charge of my future," said Pete. "I have a lot of options; I just haven't decided on the best route for me yet. But, okay, I'll play along. How do I strengthen my self-efficacy?" asked Pete.

"Bandura described it as *self-management of your inner life*.[19] In practical terms, there are four ways to enhance self-efficacy that may be helpful for you," Rick replied.

SELF-REFLECTION

Examine your intentions, your actions, and their meanings. You can develop a keener awareness of how they contribute to and influence the course of events. At times of transition, pay attention to what you're choosing to do and what it's creating for you. Start a journal and record what you're observing.

SELF-REAPPRAISAL

In times of change, some of your capabilities won't be as relevant going forward. Step back and reappraise your capabilities. Figure out how you need to adapt. Identify what adjustments you need to make in this new life of retirement. Remember to think long term. Retirement will likely make up a sizable portion of your life. It's likely to last twenty to thirty years or more.

MODELING

Observe others who are already doing what you want to do. A role model can give you a snapshot of competencies you'd need to develop. Talk with people who've retired and built a new life. You can learn a lot from their experience.

PERSEVERANCE

The best way to build self-efficacy is to take on a tough challenge, such as bouncing back from a setback or overcoming adversity. It intensifies self-efficacy because you're generating evidence that you can influence the course of events.

FORWARD THINKING

"The self-efficacy you bring from your professional life gives you a strong foundation. You just need to figure out how to adjust it for this new phase of life," Rick concluded.

"So, let me see if I'm getting this right. By taking charge of my future, because I know my actions will shape what happens, I create some certainty of my own, regain some control and neutralize uncertainty," said Pete.

"That's correct," Rick replied.

"Okay, then where do we go from here?" Pete asked.

"Let me ask you, what was the most helpful thing you learned from this session?" Rick said.

Pete thought for a minute and replied, "The idea of thinking through what I want my day-to-day life to be like. I'm ready to dive into that."

"Okay," Rick replied. "You mentioned that you want to be involved in a variety of things. I'll send you an exercise to work through next. It'll help you envision what that might look like and feel like."

Later that afternoon, Pete was at home, thinking about his discussion with Rick. He felt good about this next exercise. He was eager to get into specifics.

Pete noticed lately that both he and Bailey were eagerly awaiting Melissa's arrival from work each day. At the sound of the garage door, Bailey would drop whatever she was doing and trot over to the door. Now, Pete was doing the same.

Melissa entered with her typical burst of energy. "You'll never guess who I ran into at Starbucks this afternoon? Your old boss Jim. He said he's been trying to reach you about that guy Matt from SCORE. Matt's been trying to reach you, too."

Pete still wasn't much of a text guy. When he checked his phone, he saw two missed calls from Jim, four texts from Matt, and a text from Joanna, one of his proteges at his last company. It was marked URGENT. Pete smiled. He remembered URGENT. It wasn't part of his daily life anymore, except when Bailey ran off to his neighbor's house and barked incessantly.

Jim and Matt could wait, he figured. When he reached Joanna, he could tell he made the right call. She needed his help. Without Pete's role, she and his other former direct reports were now responsible for working directly with the sales executives. They were notoriously demanding and challenging to deal with. He learned that Joanna was handling them well, but she wanted his advice on one in particular: Pete's former nemesis. Joanna was highly capable, but she was curious about what Pete thought was her best move with a tough confrontation she was anticipating. It was a good conversation with Joanna, and Pete felt he helped her.

Next, he dialed Jim. "Finally!" said Jim. "I am *so* glad you called. Matt needs your help—it's urgent."

Wow. Urgent! Pete thought to himself. *Twice in one day. What are the odds?*

"Matt took your advice from our meeting, and it's working. He has three meetings with new potential investors coming up next week. But now he's freaking out. He's been trying to reach you. He said you left him a voicemail a few weeks ago about some new ideas. He thinks they're excellent, and he wants to add them to his deck. He wants you to text them to him ASAP."

"Ask Matt to call me and remind him that I'm old school. He has my number. We'll talk it through," said Pete.

TAKEAWAYS

1. Dealing with uncertainty is part of the reality in transitioning to retirement. It heightens anxiety and fear of the unknown.
2. Some people are less tolerant of uncertainty. It can lead them to feel stuck and unsure of where to go next because they see many options and many threats. One way to beat uncertainty is to break challenges down into smaller parts to be more doable and less overwhelming.
3. Self-efficacy positions you as the central agent of change, ultimately in control of your future direction, not your circumstances. Anyone can develop a sense of self-efficacy at any age, but it's wise to renew it as you enter transitions in life.

4. There are several ways to strengthen self-efficacy. Engage in reflection through practices like starting a journal. Reappraise your capabilities in light of the new phase of life you are entering and identify any adjustments that may be needed. Find role models who are succeeding at doing what you'd like to do. Taking on new challenges or rebounding from setbacks can powerfully impact your self-efficacy by providing proof of your capabilities.

Pete's learning many things the hard way. But you can learn from the example of others.

EXERCISE—SELF-EFFICACY

1. Who are role models doing what you'd like to do in your retirement? Identify two people you know personally and two public figures.
2. What stands out about them?
3. What one thing can you learn from them and apply to your life?
4. What competencies will you want to develop to strengthen your personal agency?
5. What will you need to adapt to in order to retire well and age well?

CHAPTER EIGHT

IGNITE THE RIGHT DEGREE OF CHALLENGE TO BATTLE COMPLACENCY

"We have a normal. As you move outside of your comfort zone, what was once the unknown and frightening becomes your new normal."

—ROBIN SHARMA

Pete's old boss Jim emailed to give him a heads-up that Matt would be calling. "Here's what you need to know," he wrote. "The first pitch meeting was a disaster. The investor scheduled an hour, and it lasted thirteen minutes. Matt must have rubbed them the wrong way from the jump. I don't think he knows why. He needs some emergency mentoring. His next pitch meeting is on Friday. It's with the biggest potential investor. The clock's ticking."

It didn't take long for Matt to call Pete this time. Jim was right. The pressure was getting to Matt. His speech was rapid-fire.

He didn't waste any time with pleasantries. Matt needed to hear Pete's ideas for his product launch *now*.

"Let me be upfront with you. I don't need your old-school guidance," Matt said. "I just need new ideas. That's all. I've got the rest covered."

Pete opted to count not just to ten but to fourteen before speaking. Eventually, the conversation turned collaborative, zeroing in on one of the ideas. Much to Pete's surprise, the call ended up lasting two hours. Their back-and-forth made Pete's initial ideas sharper. Matt was excited about it and wanted to feature it in his upcoming pitch meetings with the biggest potential investor. Pete advised him to think about it, then bounce it off a few other people first. *I'm starting to sound like Rick,* he thought.

When he got home, Pete's phone buzzed again. It was Jim again. "I don't hear from you for five years, and now I'm number one on your speed dial again?"

"Just calling to say thanks for spending the time with Matt. I don't know what you're doing, but it's a big help to him," said Jim.

"He's a bright guy and a quick study," Pete replied. "I do think he needs to smooth out some rough edges with his interpersonal skills, though. It's going to hold him back. Are you working with him on that?"

"I'm just a SCORE volunteer helping him on his business plan. You're his *mentor*. That's in your department."

"Wait. Hold on! When did I sign up for..." Pete started to say before realizing Jim had ended the call. Again.

The next morning, Pete met Matt in a coffee shop across the street from the university. The school was in the middle of mid-terms. You could sense the tension as soon as you walked in. Students had packed the place and were glued to their laptops, wired taut with caffeine. Pete spotted Matt at a table near the back. He looked sullen, cradling his cup of coffee. Pete noted that Matt did not offer to get him one, too.

Matt walked Pete through what happened at the last pitch meeting and how he was shocked it ended so quickly. Matt wasn't sure what he did wrong or how he could fix it. He confided he was nervous about his upcoming meeting with the most significant potential investor. "I know it's my last chance," Matt said. "I can't blow it this time. I know my product is *killer*. I just need someone to see that."

"Maybe so," said Pete. "But right now, *you're* the killer. I think you're killing the conversation before they can get to see how good your product is. Your message can't get through because you've turned them off. They can't hear you."

Pete walked him back through the meeting to help Matt process what had happened. It was clear that Matt didn't get it. Pete stopped him several times, asking him to freeze-frame his telling of the story to break down certain moments. Matt was annoyed, but Pete was straightforward, in a tough-love way. Suddenly it dawned on Matt what had gone wrong. He'd focused entirely on the engineering parts of his presentation.

He had not been at all attentive to the human side of the interaction.

Pete shifted Matt's focus to the upcoming meeting, asking him what he knew about the potential investor and what the investor cared most about. It quickly became apparent Matt had some homework to do. "What you need is a Scouting Report," Pete said.

When they reconvened at the coffee shop a few days later, Matt had indeed done his homework, compiling an impressive dossier on the investor. Perhaps just as impressive, he had brought Pete a cup of tea to the table this time. Over the next hour, the two worked together on how to handle the people side of the meeting.

Pete explained that while everyone else is trying to come up with the perfect elevator pitch for their product, he wanted Matt to focus on doing what Seth Godin recommends. Instead of leading with an elevator pitch, he should lead with an elevator *question*.[1] Something like: *What was the moment you knew your most successful investment was going to be a home run?* By getting investors talking first about what they care most about, you're building a connection right away.

"Let's work on those questions that will help you understand the investor better," Pete said. "What can you ask to get the investor talking first before you pitch?"

The ideas Matt came up with were good, and Pete left with a positive feeling about Matt's level of preparation.

The following day, Pete was trying to keep up with Bailey on their morning romp. He was lost in thought about Matt. The meeting was set for the next morning in New York, and Pete thought he'd call him later to check in.

Pete had let Bailey off her leash in the park, which he wasn't supposed to do. Now he was paying for it, scrambling wildly to corral her. He had almost caught her when his phone went off. Jim. Again.

"Sounds like you've got Matt ready for prime time tomorrow," he said. "There's just one problem—he needs you *at* the meeting."

"*What?*" Pete gaped.

"He told the investor he's bringing his strategic advisor. They're expecting you to be there," Jim proceeded to hang up before Pete could respond. Again.

Pete decided he would go to New York if it would help Matt. But first, he insisted they talk through what his role would be—and clearly what it would *not be*. On the big day, Pete arrived for the pitch meeting thirty minutes early. He looked up at a nondescript building in the Meatpacking District in New York City. He wondered if he may be overdressed with his Brooks Brothers blazer, blue oxford button-down, khakis, and the Samuel Hubbard shoes he always got compliments on.

As he entered the reception area at Soho House, he realized it was the opposite. He was underdressed and way out of his fashion league.

Soho House is an exclusive members-only club for creatives, with a waiting list of over 25,000. The New York club is skewed toward the fashion industry, musicians, actors and actresses, and some successful businesspeople. Pete recognized a few actors, two pop singers, and a rapper watching him from the reception area.

Matt's potential investor must have serious sway at Soho House given that they had made a special exception for Pete to bring Bailey along as well. He hadn't been able to find anyone to watch her, and now Bailey was enjoying the new sights, sounds, and smells of their big-city adventure. She also seemed to have star quality because within minutes of arriving, she was surrounded by three models asking if it was okay to pet her.

Pete was pleasantly surprised to see Matt had arrived even earlier than he did. Unlike Pete, he had dressed the part. He looked like he fit in there, and he seemed comfortable and confident.

They were escorted to their table in the main room. Matt and Pete took their seats, and a striking woman named Sarah approached their table. Pete recognized her instantly from Matt's dossier. She was a wealthy angel investor from Silicon Valley who was in New York for the week. Sarah had founded a tech start-up fifteen years earlier that Google bought for a considerable amount. As Matt had discovered in his research, she was also a big dog lover. Bailey hit it off with her right away and, much to Pete's surprise, took her place at Sarah's side.

Sarah signaled it was time to get down to business, stressing she had another commitment in thirty minutes. Matt opened with his elevator question: *Which of your investments have had the greatest impact on the world so far?* It worked perfectly. The question took Sarah by surprise, Pete thought, but it got her talking about why she did what she did. From there, Matt took her through his deck and his product. Sarah was savvy and drilled down on the key technical elements. She poked holes in his design, strategy, and production plan, testing areas of weakness.

Once she had exhausted her questions, she turned to Pete and asked him with a smile, "Since you're his strategic advisor, what's the one question he doesn't want me to ask?" Pete felt her gaze and knew he was squarely on the spot.

"I'd ask about his marketing plan," Pete said after a brief pause. "It's still a work in progress, and it's critically important." Sarah did just that. Matt handled her inquiries reasonably well, then solicited her marketing advice. At precisely the thirty-minute mark, she abruptly rose and shook hands with Matt, saying, "My team will be in touch."

Her vacated space was filled quickly by a well-known actress from a popular TV series who wanted to hang out with Bailey. Matt just stared blankly ahead, unsure of what had just taken place.

SCOUTING REPORT: BATTLING COMPLACENCY

The next day, Pete was putting the finishing touches on the scouting report for his upcoming meeting with Rick. He wanted to go a different route with this one and decided to shoot a video, albeit with a great deal of technical guidance from his daughter Anne.

CHALLENGE VERSUS COMPLACENCY

The opening scene was a clip of an economics professor at George Mason University, Tyler Cowen. He was being interviewed about his book *The Complacent Class*.[2] Cowen was arguing that due to prosperity and gains in technology, a growing segment of the American populace had become accustomed to a life that was overly comfortable, convenient, and somewhat sheltered. The complacent life has consequences, Cowen noted. There was an increased resistance among this segment of the population to anything "new, different, or challenging."[3] *Why?* the interviewer asked. The professor answered that life is perhaps *too* good in the comfort zone. The data show that "15 to 20 percent of the American population is doing extraordinarily well in terms of income and social indicators, such as happiness and health outcomes."[4]

"Life begins at the edge of your comfort zone."[5]

—NEALE DONALD WALSCH

In the next shot, Pete took center stage. "Today's match is challenge versus complacency," he began, "and you might be wondering what challenge has to do with retirement. After all, you got your fill of challenge during your full-time working days, right? Those days gave you a lengthy list of accomplishments to be proud of, but those days are over. But now, you're content with where you are. You don't have to push it anymore."

"But let's take a look at the scouting report, just for fun." In the video, Pete had moved to a whiteboard. "You know the deal. We always nail down our definitions first." He wrote:

Complacency is self-satisfaction, especially when accompanied by unawareness of actual dangers or deficiencies, an instance of uninformed self-satisfaction.[6]

"It's an overall sense of satisfaction with the status quo," Pete summed up, "but with a smug attitude."

He went on to explain how complacency tries to trick you into thinking you're unique. When you are complacent, you think many things around you need to change, but there's no way you have to change as well. You like things the way they are. If you could freeze-frame everything, you would. "But a complacent life is lacking something—challenge," Pete continued. "It's missing the desire to push yourself to do your best at something. Complacency leads you to stop trying to reach your human potential. You stop pushing yourself. That attitude leaves you blind to some things."

"Blind to what?" Rick wanted to know.

Pete paused the video and explained, "You become blind to the fact that most things around you are evolving—everything except you. Complacency has led you to maintain, not grow. You're not trying to get anywhere. You lose a sense of adventure."

SERIOUS LEISURE

Pete restarted his video. "You want to have fun in retirement, right?" he said, over clips of people kicking back watching TV, going to the movies, and relaxing at the beach. "You deserve it. You've earned the right to your life of leisure. But here's what I learned in preparing this scouting report. There's a lot of research on leisure! That's what I'll be in my next life—a leisure researcher."

It turns out that there are different types of leisure. Robert Stebbins, an academic researcher who's written numerous books and peer-reviewed papers on the subject, distinguishes between three types:

DIFFERENT TYPES OF LEISURE[7]

1. *Casual Leisure.* Pure fun, informal and enjoyable right from the jump. It doesn't take much preparation or special training.

2. *Project-Based Leisure.* Something you're involved in occasionally, and it doesn't require any type of long-term commitment. It may be an annual local event you're involved in planning or even a one-off special project.

3. *Serious Leisure.* It requires more frequent and sustained involvement and generates greater rewards, including a sense of personal fulfillment.

The first two types of leisure are beneficial. There's not much of a challenge involved, at least not the kind of challenge that stretches you. The third kind, Serious Leisure, at first glance, seems like an oxymoron. But this is a way to beat complacency. It's different from the first two forms of leisure. You feel like you're working toward your potential as a human being. Stebbins, who's worked on this concept since 1973, has renamed it Serious *Pursuits* to reflect this self-actualization element.[8]

According to Stebbins, people engage in a wide range of activities related to Serious Pursuits. There are Amateurs, who are creating art, competing in athletic events, or performing music. There are Hobbyists, who are serious collectors or makers of complicated models, for example. Finally, there are Volunteers, who are supporting causes and organizations they care deeply about in the nonprofit sector.[9]

Serious Pursuits can benefit people in retirement by providing a stronger sense of well-being and self-fulfillment as well as a positive attitude.[10] Many Serious Pursuits are not solitary endeavors. They open the doors to new social relationships, and in some cases, even second careers.[11]

ANOTHER LEG TO STAND ON

And these aren't things that you have to wait until you're retired to do. A significant outside interest can add value during a career and even cushion the transition to retirement later. A recent study highlighted CEOs whose Serious Pursuits provide a valuable buffer and stress management tool.[12]

A qualitative study of sixteen large company CEOs by Emilia

Bunea validated the benefits of serious leisure and uncovered additional advantages. Participants reported a primary benefit was how serious leisure helped take their minds off work for some time. The CEOs also reported engagement with serious leisure led to increased humility, self-confidence, creativity, and wisdom.[13]

But the most striking benefit was related to crafting a new identity, one that was independent of their job. They reported describing themselves as more multidimensional: "I'm a CEO *and* a (marathon runner), (competitive cyclist), or (singer)." This additional identity added an extra dimension to how they saw themselves. Bunea, a former CEO herself, described it as a crucial asset, because CEOs' jobs are inevitably threatened or eventually come to an end. She reported one participant said that his outside pursuit gave him an extra leg to stand on.[14]

Pete paused the video because Rick had his hand raised to ask another question.

"I understand the benefits," Rick said, "but did her study shed any light on what *creates* the benefits?"

"Yes, Bunea found the CEOs' outside interest provided them a sense of control and freedom from their professional role, which was often previously all-consuming and filled with pressure from many sides,"[15] Pete explained.

For the next section of the video, Pete had interviewed four people he knew who were deeply involved in serious leisure. He also filmed conversations with four other retired people, who he suspected probably didn't have any Serious Pursuits. It wasn't a scientific study by any stretch, but Pete thought just seeing clips of the conversations brought Bunea's research to life. Pete asked them the same questions the study had posed in the exact same way.

It wasn't what the eight people said that struck Pete—it was the way they said it. The people who had Serious Pursuits were full of life. There was a passion they exhibited as they talked about what they did. In contrast, the four with more casual interests sounded content, but they were more subdued.

Among those engaged in Serious Pursuits was Cindy, a former senior executive in finance, who had taken up running in her forties and run twelve marathons. She's still competing in her sixties. "I started running 5K races with friends for various charities, and over time, I got more and more involved in running. My 'personal best' days are behind me now. These days, I'm competing with myself. But I truly enjoy the whole process of training and pushing myself to do my best. The nine months of training for each race is a story in and of itself. Each time I begin training, I wonder, *Can I still do this?* It's the challenge, I think, that keeps me coming back. It's also the people I train with in the local runner's group that are important for me. I found my new tribe that way."

Next, Pete showed a clip of Barry, who was a serious hobbyist and collected rare antique clocks. He talked about the pleasure he derived from the hunt in locating difficult-to-find timepieces. He spoke glowingly about the relationships he's developed with people all over the world who share his passion. "As you might imagine, this isn't exactly a common pursuit. But those of us who do this are really into it, and we have a lot in common."

Finally, the video highlighted Patricia, who volunteers training Labrador Retrievers for The Seeing Eye, an organization providing guide dogs for the blind. Many of the dogs she trained were now paired with sight-impaired people across the US. She spoke about her satisfaction with doing something that significantly helped people she'd never meet.

Getting involved wasn't her idea at first. Her daughter Rebecca, in seventh grade, had asked to raise one of the puppies as her Christmas gift that year. Despite her husband's initial reluctance, they decided to say yes. Her involvement with the organization has grown over time, and today, she runs the local chapter and oversees the training of the other puppy raisers.

LIFELONG LEARNING

Pete's video continued. "And then there's Lifelong Learning. Challenge inspires you to keep learning, like Curiosity does, but to apply more disciplined effort. Think of Curiosity as the spark. Challenge takes your learning to a more formal and structured level for topics you're really interested in. It knocks you off your high horse by getting you to start from square one with something new. Exhibit A is me in art class."

The research is consistent with Pete's experience. A study of over 4,400 adults, who took courses at twelve Osher Lifelong Learning Institutes in the US, cited multiple benefits from ongoing learning. The most frequently mentioned were the insights they gained from learning and the social benefits created in the learning community.[16]

MASTERY

Serious leisure and lifelong learning can add just the right degree of challenge to ward off complacency. Through either of those avenues, you might discover something that captivates you in such a way that you develop a deeper interest. You may even find yourself wanting to get so good at the pursuit that you master it, which can boost your satisfaction in retirement. Research has found that developing a sense of mastery is associated with higher self-esteem in men and fewer symptoms of depression in both women and men.[17] Mastery is more highly correlated with adjustment and satisfaction in retirement than the level of pre-retirement planning someone does.[18] Serious leisure, lifelong learning, and mastery may add a missing ingredient that makes all the difference.

THE TALK

It was finally here—Pete and Melissa's three-day weekend trip to The Catskills in New York State. The weather and fall foliage were spectacular. The couple went on two long hikes, explored the local town, and had a great dinner at a farm-to-table restaurant. It featured the tastiest vegan food Pete had ever eaten.

They were having a great time. But Pete did want to broach the subject of Melissa's thoughts on her life in retirement. He thought he had a good sense of what she'd say. *Maybe Melissa is thinking about scaling things back at the law firm soon. She always liked Oregon, Colorado, and Arizona. Maybe we'll move to one of those states,* he thought. *Thank goodness I know what she likes. She's probably jealous of my early retirement life now and can't wait to join me.*

While he thought he knew what she would say, Pete found himself procrastinating. Maybe he wasn't so sure after all? Then, on the third day of the trip, Pete and Melissa awoke to a driving rain pounding on the roof. Pete checked his weather app and saw the forecast simply said *monsoon*. He was never so happy to see so much rain. Today would be perfect for their talk.

After breakfast, Pete started a fire, and they curled up with their respective books, hunkered down for a relaxing day together indoors. To Pete's surprise, Melissa broached the subject first.

"Wasn't there something you wanted to talk to me about for your work with Rick?" asked Melissa.

"There is something I'd like to discuss, but it's not for Rick," Pete said. "It's for me. For *us*, really.

"Now that I'm in this early retirement life, I'm wondering when you think *you'll* be ready to retire. What do you think you'll want to do when you do retire?"

Melissa laughed. "Oh, I see. So, now you're doing business development for Rick? I'm his next victim?"

"No. Nothing like that. It just dawned on me that we haven't talked much about it. And I'm curious about what you think," answered Pete.

"Well, I haven't given it that much thought," Melissa began. "First, we had the pandemic. Then what happened to you with your job was such a big surprise. And then you deciding to retire early was an even bigger surprise. But when to retire is not a top-of-mind question for me. I love my work. I'm making up for lost time in my career. And I want to see how things sort out for you. I want you to be happy."

"But what makes *you* happy?" asked Pete.

"I'm not sure you understand how important my work at the law firm is for me, Pete," answered Melissa. "Especially now. We've never been empty nesters before, and now Andy and Anne are off at college. It's the first time I can really go for it at work without all the juggling I used to do. I'm getting more responsibility now. I feel like the next five to ten years will be my prime, and I want to make the most of them."

"*Years?*" interjected Pete.

"Absolutely," answered Melissa. "I don't know why that surprises you. I'm not ready to slow down. Without the kids at home, I'm ready to speed up."

"Sounds like you're leaving me in the dust," said Pete, laughing.

"No, that's silly. You have all the things you're doing, and that's great. And I can see it's been good for you, even if you're still figuring it all out. But I love what I'm doing. I want to see this through at work."

"Okay," said Pete. "You've always supported what I want to do."

"We've always supported each other," corrected Melissa.

"So, no changes then. We'll keep doing our own thing. Maybe, we should talk about this again in a couple of years," said Pete, on his way to the kitchen to fetch another cup of coffee.

"Not so fast, Sparky," Melissa added. "I'd like to talk about maybe moving back to the city."

"Moving?" replied Pete, frozen in mid-stride.

"Yes," Melissa said. "I know you love where we live, but it's *way* too much house for just the two of us. And wouldn't it be great to move back into the city? Remember how much you loved it?"

"Us? Now? City?" stammered Pete. This was not at all what he expected.

"C'mon, Pete. It'll be fun! A new adventure," Melissa said with a smile.

"We'll have to see what Bailey thinks" was all he could come up with at the moment.

Later that afternoon, on her iPad Melissa showed Pete multiple options they might like in the city. She pointed out the unique opportunity presented by the dynamics of the real estate market. Demand was high for homes like theirs in the suburbs, as people had been leaving the city in droves, and the market in the city hadn't been so low in over ten years.

It took a while, but Pete was beginning to slightly warm up to the idea. But he'd need more time to think about this one.

He remembered the other part of the assignment from Rick was to find out what Melissa's expectations were of him. As the rain ended and the sun returned, they went for a walk into town.

Melissa's first response was a variation on what she had said earlier. "I just expect you to be happy." But Pete pressed her with a few "Rick questions" he had in his back pocket:

What could I do More of?

What could I do Less of?

He instantly regretted it. Melissa's answers were swift and specific. His to-do list was stacking up. He was getting a headache fast.

The big issue centered around Pete doing more around the house. Much more. *Ouch.*

Melissa argued that while Pete was now home virtually all the time, she still handled most of the work at home. While Pete began to protest that he had indeed been doing more, he quickly realized it wasn't near his share. He asked Melissa, "Okay. What would be the one thing that would be the most helpful?"

"That's easy," she replied. "Make dinner more often. That would be a huge step forward. I wouldn't have to get takeout so often. It'll be better for both of us."

Later that day, traffic was light on the way home, and the

drive was pleasant. But as they pulled into the driveway, Pete realized he had some recalibrating to do.

TAKEAWAYS

1. Rethink how you could use your free time, even while you're still in your full-time working years. Investigate different areas of interest, including things you used to love doing. Experiment with other options. One may evolve into a Serious Pursuit, offering multiple benefits, including fulfillment and new social relationships.
2. Don't stand pat. Explore opportunities for Lifelong Learning. Start small, but force yourself out of your comfort zone and add the right level of challenge into your life.
3. Alignment matters. If you're married or in a relationship, talk with your spouse or partner about their hopes, dreams, and fears about retirement. Their answers may surprise you. Talking about where you may want to live in retirement can be especially useful as it unveils core values and what's most important to each of you at this stage of life.

You can have too much of a good thing. When you're immersed in full-time work, a life of leisure looks wonderful. But for many people, after a while, it lacks something. Let's look at what you might take up in retirement that would push you a little and add the right degree of Challenge:

EXERCISE—FIND THE RIGHT LEVEL OF CHALLENGE IN RETIREMENT

1. What interests could become Serious Pursuits for you in retirement?

2. Take a look at the various activities at https://www.seriousleisure.net/. Which pique your interest?
3. How can you try one or more of those activities?
4. What's one thing you could master in retirement?

CHAPTER NINE

PURSUE A CALLING AND TRANSCEND OBLIGATIONS

"The highest calling is to grow into our authentic selfhood, whether or not it conforms to what others think it ought to be."[1]

—PARKER PALMER

Pete was thinking about the upside to moving back to the city. The convenience factor was at the top of his list. They'd be able to walk to more places. Plus, he always had found the buzz of city life appealing. But Melissa's enthusiasm for the move far exceeded his own. He tried to focus on the positives but found himself always returning to the things he'd miss. He loved their current home, their friendly neighborhood, and their favorite restaurants. He'd even miss his neighbor Dave's endless lawn mowing.

When he thought like this, the memories would inevitably begin to flow. Andy's and Anne's first steps. Learning to read. Bike rides. Basketball games. Waffles and ice cream for breakfast on the first day of school each year. Movie night. Game night. The day they brought Bailey home as a puppy. All the holidays. Halloween, especially the year he dressed up in a giant Teletubbies costume, which he still has not lived down. He wondered, *Why are we leaving such a special place? It's been such a big part of our lives.*

Pete's stroll down memory lane was interrupted by his ringing phone. It was Joanna, his former direct report. She called to thank him for the advice he had offered the last time they had spoken. "I can't tell you how valuable it was. It helped me see things from a different point of view. And I was wondering, would you be up for being my mentor? It would mean a lot to me."

"I'd be honored," replied Pete. "But only on one condition." Pete had always appreciated Joanna's abilities. Perhaps she hadn't realized it, but Joanna was the one he would go to when he needed a sense of a situation and the interpersonal dynamics. "It will have to be a mutual mentorship. There's a lot I can learn from you. Right now, I'm helping this younger entrepreneur Matt. I can use your help in bridging the generation gap sometimes."

The conversation reminded him he hadn't heard from Matt since their meeting in New York. Pete made a note to reach out to him. Joanna agreed to talk further next week. At the moment, Pete had an urgent matter to attend to—it was time for Bailey's walk. He needed time to think about his homework while they walked through the park, another thing he would surely miss.

SCOUTING REPORT: PURSUING A CALLING

Pete was puzzled by Rick's next assignment. They agreed to split the upcoming scouting report. Pete's section was about discovering your calling. "Do you think he's trying to tell me something, Bailey?" Pete asked. Bailey cocked her head to one side. "Yeah. You're right. He's *always* trying to tell me something."

There would be no slide deck or video this time. Pete came to the meeting with Rick with six pages of handwritten notes and questions for Rick.

"What did you find out about discovering a calling?" Rick asked after Pete had settled into his chair.

"Well, I was surprised to see this topic. It's a little *woo-woo* for you, Rick. It made me wonder if you think I should be thinking about being a monk or considering the priesthood or something."

"Those are paths for some people, though probably not for you," Rick said with a chuckle. "But it is helpful to explore multiple avenues. Some callings are indeed spiritual in their focus, but many are not."

"Yes. *Now* I know that," said Pete.

"Are you ready to share what you've found?" asked Rick.

"Of course," said Pete. "You know I always do my homework."

"Where should we start?" asked Rick.

"So, this topic is new to me," said Pete. "I've never really thought about being *called* to do something."

WHAT IS A CALLING?

Having a calling isn't as rare as you might think. One study found about 35 percent of people feel they have a calling.[2]

A calling is doing work out of a sense of inner direction—work that would contribute to a better world.[3]

Callings are invitations from life to serve, to activate your will toward a cause worthy of you and the human family.[4] A calling is creating a sense of meaning by uniting the self with something larger.[5] A calling is about getting involved with something beyond yourself, something that's meaningful, to others and to you. You're pulled toward doing something for the greater good. A calling aligns with a sense of a person's purpose in life.[6]

THE MINDSET OF A CALLING

Individual perspective on how people see what they do makes a big difference. There's an old story about how different people can be doing precisely the same thing and whereas it's just a task for one person, for another, it's a calling. For example, a couple on vacation were walking up a hill in San Francisco. They encountered three people working on the construction of a new building. The wife was an architect and curious about what was being built. She asked the first worker his job.

He was visibly annoyed about being interrupted. He barked, "What does it look like? I'm cutting stones." She thought he heard the worker grumble "Idiots!" as he walked away. The couple continued up the hill.

Soon, they came across a second worker doing the same task. He was also busy but looked more approachable. She asked him the same question. The worker paused, just for a moment, and explained, "I am a professional stonecutter. I'm hired for my specialized skills. But to be honest with you, as soon as I receive my check at the end of next month, I'll be heading back home and on to another job." The worker smiled and turned his attention back to his work. The couple thanked him and continued up the hill.

Toward the top of the hill, they saw a third worker. He was also doing the same tasks. As they drew near, he put down his tools and walked over to introduce himself. The architect asked him the same question about what he was doing. He smiled broadly and answered, "Well, I am building a cathedral." He explained, "I've traveled far to be part of this team, and I miss my family terribly. But I know the vision for this building. It will be a special place for many people for a long time. How it turns out for the community depends on the quality of the work we're doing right now."

A calling isn't limited to *paid* work. Studies of people following a calling in different areas such as volunteering, parenting, grandparenting, and leisure pursuits found that people with a calling report a higher degree of fulfillment in their lives, whether it's paid employment or activities outside of paid work.[7]

CALLINGS IN RETIREMENT?

One study asked retirees to describe their retirement using different metaphors. Some called it a Renaissance, a time to pursue multiple passions. Others portrayed retirement as an opportunity for Transformation. For them, it's a time to discover new ways to use the skills they've developed but in service to others.[8] Another study focused explicitly on callings in retirement. There were 196 participants, age fifty-one and older, who were retired for a year or more. Seventy-nine percent reported that they perceived they had a calling. There were different types of callings, including:[9]

- Helping Others (39 percent)
- Family/Caregiving (12 percent)
- Investment in Self/Personal Development (12 percent)
- Arts (9 percent)
- Teaching (8 percent)

However, pursuing a calling in retirement is not something everyone wants to do or can do. Common obstacles include resources, health issues, and caregiving responsibilities. Interestingly, caregiving showed up as both an obstacle *and* a calling. Like the stonecutters, some people see caregiving responsibilities as an obligation, while others see it as part of their purpose.

OBLIGATIONS

"So, who's our adversary this time?" asked Pete.

"It's a tough one," replied Rick. "We see it as external to us, but it's really within us."

"So, it's like one of those Halloween movies. The call is coming from inside the house?" said Pete.

"Something like that," answered Rick. "We all have responsibilities and commitments. Some are non-negotiable. I'm not talking about those. But as we learned earlier, the expectations of other people can have an outsized impact on us. They feel like a weight on us, but it's really about the importance we give them.

"Some responsibilities can feel like an obligation over time. Sometimes, these negotiable obligations need to be evaluated mindfully and adjusted. Sometimes, it's time to say no to others so you can say yes to yourself."

"I can see that," said Pete. "But can't obligations be a good thing? Can't they motivate us, help us strive for more, reach higher than we thought was possible? Be the best we can be? Leap tall buildings in a single bound?"

"Slow down," said Rick. "Yes. Obligations can be helpful in many ways, but they can also keep us from our true calling."

"How?" asked Pete.

"They can keep you in a job, in a career, or at a company that's not right for you for too long. Obligations make you feel like you don't have any choice. In some cases, that may be true. But in other cases, you have more choice than you realize.

"The best evidence I can give you comes from Bronnie Ware. She was a palliative care counselor in Australia and wrote a book about her conversations with the critically ill, *The Top Five Regrets of the Dying*. Here is the regret people expressed most often," Rick said as he wrote on his whiteboard:

"I wish I'd dared to live a life true to myself, not the life others expected of me."[10]

"There's a lot in that single sentence. Let's unpack it for a minute," suggested Rick. "What jumped out at you?"

"Well, the first thing is the phrase *a life true to myself.* I guess that's what life is ultimately all about," replied Pete.

"What else?" asked Rick.

"The last part," said Pete. "I can see how what others expected of me came to feel like an obligation. They were choices I made. And I didn't ever re-examine or re-negotiate them. They felt like a burden I had put on myself. And it became harder and harder to get out from under them."

"What else?" asked Rick.

"Courage," answered Pete. "That's where I get stuck. It takes real courage to say no and then go your own way. Other people may disapprove of your choice if it's something that goes against the grain."

Rick nodded and shared a saying from psychologist and author Wayne Dyer related to the story of Ivan Ilyich by Leo Tolstoy:

Don't die with your music still inside you.[11]

DISCOVERING A CALLING

"So, how do people discover their calling?" asked Rick.

"I came into this thinking it was a 'bolt from the blue' kind of thing. But I read in the research that it's usually an ongoing process," said Pete.

The executive coach and teacher John Schuster advises looking at the various roles you've taken on to discern the themes of your life. He recommends looking at your past to identify the different callings you've already responded to and which ones you've ignored. He refers to it as reviewing your Call History. He says some calls are persistent, and a review may help you tune in to a recurring call you left to simmer on a back burner.[12]

Rick had given Pete an exercise to complete. In this exercise, you picture yourself at a dinner party. There are six guests who have been invited. All of the invited guests are other versions of You. These versions of You are who you would have become if you had made different choices and followed other paths. Then, you pay attention to which versions you chose to spend the most time with at the dinner party and which ones you avoided.[13]

"What did you learn from the dinner party exercise?" asked Rick.

"There were versions of Me that I would regret. One was Me

if I hadn't met and married Melissa. I avoided him. And there was a version of Me if we didn't have children. That was a very self-absorbed version of Me. I couldn't wait to move away from him. Then there were a few 'What If?' versions. The one I spent a lot of time with was the *What If My College Choice Wasn't Solely Based on Where I Could Play Basketball?* version. He was a much smarter version of me, I must say. But the most interesting was the *What If I Chose a Different Career Path?* one. He's done a lot of different things. And he has me wondering about new possibilities in my early retirement."

"You have one more guest to invite to your next dinner party," said Rick.

"Next time, invite Future You. I'd like to hear what he's like. He'll also help you understand how to keep obligations from impacting your choices."

LEARNING FROM SILENCE

"So, what's the biggest thing you learned about how to beat Obligations and do what you were truly meant to do?" asked Rick.

"I read about how reflection helps in discovering what you were meant to do. The most common way people find their calling is through silence," explained Pete. "When you're constantly on the go, you're rarely quiet enough to hear a calling. You're surrounded by so much noise. It's hard to pick up the signal."

Dave Isay, founder of StoryCorps, an organization that has

recorded over 65,000 stories across the US, wrote: "Finding what you're meant to do with your life has a lot to do with careful listening—to that quiet voice inside that speaks to who you truly are."[14]

> *"Listen past the constant drumbeat of social noise. Listen to what you truly want to do."*[15]
>
> —JOHN SCHUSTER

Identity can be a limiting factor. It is often rooted in the work you do, and it can leave you less open to other possibilities. Some people see themselves as synonymous with their jobs, especially men. They may perceive themselves as having obligations to their profession and their identity.[16] People who find a calling report having an open mind and spending time regularly in quiet reflection listening to that inner voice—the one we all have but often ignore.[17] But if you do hear a call, focus on the direction and take some action. Artist, entrepreneur, and photographer Chase Jarvis advises tuning in to hear a call, then simply start moving toward it. Start the journey and figure it out as you go.[18]

"Have you had clients who found their calling heading into retirement?" asked Pete.

"Yes. Not all do, but some do, yes," replied Rick.

"How did they go about it?" Pete asked.

"Let me share two different stories. They're not clients, but they're two people I've talked with, and these may be helpful," Rick said.

TWO CASES OF CALLINGS

Some callings are spiritually driven. Take Steve Javie. Steve was a top-rated referee in the National Basketball Association for twenty-five years, officiating over 1,500 regular-season games and 243 playoff games, including twenty-three NBA Finals games. He's an ESPN analyst these days, but that's only part of what he's up to. A troublesome knee led him to retire from the NBA in 2011. But a year before he retired, after enduring a series of knee surgeries, he described his prayer experience where he proposed a deal.[19]

"Look, if you give me my twenty-fifth year, I'm all yours, whatever you want from me," Steve recalled praying. "I was going to daily Mass at the time anyway, and my relationship with the Lord was good. I just didn't know where I was going in my life after officiating. And darn it, didn't you know, He gave me my twenty-fifth year. When I came back for that last season, my knees started wearing out again by the end of the year. And I knew this was it, but it was like, the Lord gave me a gift. And then, you know, I have to keep my end of the bargain."

For months after he retired, he kept up his prayer practice. "'Show me the way to make sure my heart and my eyes are open to what You have planned for me, whatever it may be.' I had no idea. And so, my wife and I went to a presentation by Jeff Cavins, who's a world-renowned Catholic speaker. He talked about how God speaks to you. Now, mind you, I'd been praying for six months, seven months now, for God to speak to me. And I'm listening to Cavins say that. And I go, 'Yeah, buddy, He might speak to you. He's not speaking to me.' At that very moment, that word 'deacon' came into my mind. Now, I didn't know what a deacon did. We had a couple of deacons at our parish, *but what do they do?* I wondered. *How do you go about becoming one?* I had no idea. But I couldn't get this word *deacon* out of my mind. I told my wife about it after the presentation as we were going home. And she said, 'You better talk to my senior pastor about what's going on.' And this is how the calling all started. It started in prayer. It started when I guess my heart was open, and my ears were open to listen."

After a seven-year course of study and discernment in the Archdiocese of Philadelphia, Steve was ordained as a deacon in the Catholic Church in 2019. He serves today in St. Andrews parish in Newtown, Pennsylvania. It's a new rewarding life with a spiritual focus that he didn't see coming. Keep an open mind about your future. An unexpected direction can open up if you're attuned to it.

Serendipity also played a role in Melissa Davey's future.[20] She was a vice president at a national company for twenty-five years, in her mid-sixties, and beginning to ask, *What's next?* Should she re-up for another five-year contract, retire, or do something else entirely? One thing on her mind was all the creative things she wished she had done. The one that kept recurring was filmmaking. She'd always felt drawn to it, but she dismissed it as an unrealistic possibility at her stage of life.

One day, a car drive in the Pennsylvania countryside with a friend led to a chance encounter with a crew filming in a field.

Following a hunch, Melissa's quick web search confirmed it was a project of director M. Night Shyamalan, who was filming a micro-budget movie. On his website was an auction for his educational foundation to win a day on the set with him. Melissa's friend encouraged her to bid, which she did and she won. She spent a full day on the set, learning how he went about filmmaking, including detailed insight into his thinking behind various approaches to different scenes and shots.

A series of questions from the director himself at the end of the day was the highlight. Shyamalan asked about what Melissa did for a living and followed up with more questions to better understand her job. Melissa explains what happened next:

"He looked at me curiously with kind of this twinkle in his eye. He said, 'What do you *really* want to do?' My immediate response was, 'Well, I want your job.' His immediate response was, 'Well, you'd better hurry up then.'"

The conversation prompted Melissa to follow her calling. She resigned the next day and embarked on a journey to create a documentary film titled *The Beyond Sixty Project*, chronicling the lives of nine extraordinary women in the US.

Reflecting on the lessons she learned from crafting an award-winning film, Melissa explained that your inner voice can lead you to your calling, but you also have to know when to ignore it when it turns critical:

"To leave the earth with lots of unfinished business, I think it would be a sad thing. So, I encourage people not to let their fear take over, not to listen to that little person in their head, saying, *You can't do this; you're too old*. Just totally ignore that and go find people that you can talk to that will support you."

A calling can be spiritually based or not. Sometimes it evolves over a long period of discernment. Other times, serendipity can spur you toward a path that's long been forming. The common threads are careful listening and having an open mind and heart.

"Thank you, Rick. This gives me a lot to think about," said Pete. "Before I go, I have something else for you."

It was another painting from art class. As opposed to the first one, in which Pete was suspended in mid-air surrounded by dense fog, the fog had cleared in this new one, and Pete had his two feet planted firmly on the ground. He was looking off into the distance into a beautiful vista.

"What are you calling this one?" Rick asked.

"*New Horizons*," answered Pete. "There are only four more classes, and we're already starting work on our last painting. I see my future more clearly now. I just have to evaluate my options and know where I want to experiment."

TAKEAWAYS

1. A calling is something you become engaged with that creates meaning for you and contributes to the greater good.
2. Callings can be either paid work or unpaid work. More people report having a calling than you might expect. Call-

ings are sometimes pursued in retirement, and retirees today are pursuing a wide range of callings.

3. Callings are usually discovered over time through careful listening. To hear a calling, create some quiet, reflective time away from the whirl of daily life and tune into your inner voice.

EXERCISE: WHAT'S CALLED YOU—AND WHAT'S CALLING YOU NOW?

Sometimes it's hard to discern a calling for a second act clearly in the busy whirl of working life. Check in along with Pete on what might be calling you and, just for fun, host a dinner with Future You.

1. What's your Call History? Which callings have you answered over the years?
2. Which callings have you ignored?
3. Is there an unanswered call that speaks to you now?
4. Invite six versions of you, including Future You, to a dinner party. What did you notice about the versions of you who turned out differently because they followed other paths?
5. What did you learn from Future You? What path did he or she choose?

CHAPTER TEN

THE UNBEATENS: JOY, GRATITUDE, AND HUMOR

"You don't usually hear the words joy and retirement together. So, try to shake that paradigm a little bit to say this has the potential to be the most joyful period of our lives."[1]

—HELEN DENNIS

After his visit with Rick, Pete and Melissa drove to Little Squam Lake in New Hampshire to visit Melissa's favorite aunt, Aunt Al, as they called her, short for Alberta. They always had a great time seeing Aunt Al and Melissa's cousins Jane and Patty, Jane's husband Marco, and their son Jac from Miami. Melissa was curious about how Pete thought things were going with Rick. Pete knew Melissa, as a lawyer, was skeptical about many things. Now she was drilling into the endgame.

"So, when do you, shall we say, graduate?"

"Pretty soon," Pete said. "Our last meeting is next month. The coaching process ends, but I think that just begins the next leg of my journey. It's been beneficial."

"Good," said Melissa. "Don't you usually have a topic you focus on each session? What's the area of focus for the last session?"

"I don't know yet. Rick usually sends me the homework ahead of time. I'm sure I'll get something soon."

"I know you've covered a lot of ground, but how do you know you and Rick aren't missing something?" asked Melissa. "Maybe there's something important you're not discussing."

"I seriously doubt it. I trust Rick. But I'm always open to other opinions," said Pete.

"Always?" asked Melissa with a smile.

"From certain people, of course. What do you have in mind?"

"I'm just wondering if you should get an additional perspective. I don't mean another coach. Maybe someone who's gone through retirement and has some other lessons learned. Maybe someone older and even wiser than Rick?" added Melissa.

"Who do you have in mind?" Pete asked.

"I'll have to think about it. Who's the wisest person we know?" Melissa asked.

The answer came quickly to both of them.

Aunt Al had always been Melissa's favorite. They shared the same temperament. Positive and pragmatic. A combination of optimism and skepticism. They were "trust but verify" types. Nothing got past them.

Aunt Al laughed when Jane explained that Pete had decided to retire early. "Isn't that wonderful, Mom?" Jane asked.

"Pete, you're way too young to retire!" Alberta said. "You'll be bored silly."

Melissa explained how Pete had been working with a coach and was building a plan.

Pete jumped in: "And while I'm pleased with what I've worked on with my coach, Melissa's concerned that we might be missing something. I'd love to get your advice, Aunt Al."

THE UNBEATENS

After listening to what Pete had learned so far, Aunt Al was ready to offer her own insight.

"There are three other things you'll want on your side in retirement, besides financial security, of course. The first is joy," said Aunt Al. "You're surrounded by it if you know where to look. Take the time to notice, appreciate, and celebrate things. Did you ever notice how easy it is for kids to express joy in the moment? Somehow, we lose that. Try to notice those small moments in daily living. They are special, and retirement gives you the space and the pace to enjoy them fully. You own your time. Fill it with joy as much as you can.

"The second one is gratitude," continued Aunt Al. "Appreciate the gifts you have. Reflect on them often. Some of my friends who have had so much good fortune waste a lot of time complaining about minor things. And frankly, there's plenty to complain about as you get older, Pete. You'll see if you're lucky. But I think it's better to approach each day with gratitude for what you have. It doesn't take much time. Then go off and live the day. You won't be able to do that forever.

"The last one won't surprise you," she went on. "It's humor. Lighten up. Don't take things so seriously. Especially yourself. Get over yourself and see the comical side of life, especially when things go wrong. When others complain, you can laugh instead. There's an entertaining angle in most situations. I also urge you to experiment with things until you find what you truly love. It sounds easy, but it's not. Look back at what you used to love and wished you had time to do. Now you have time. Take advantage of it."

AN UNEXPECTED SCOUTING REPORT

On Sunday, Pete was surprised when Melissa asked him to drive home. She loathed his driving and always preferred to be at the wheel. But as soon as they turned onto the highway, the reason became clear. Melissa had fired up her laptop and jumped into her work. Pete knew to give her space when she was in *law firm mode*. He figured she must have a deadline to meet, so he settled into the drive. It was an opportunity to savor the late fall foliage and collect his thoughts.

Pete smiled as he thought about how he and Melissa had

always been comfortable in silence together. As they hit the three-hour mark, he glanced over to check in.

"Ready to make a pit stop? It looks like you're deep into something. Let me guess, reviewing depositions?"

"No, it's not work-related," Melissa replied. "Some of those things Aunt Al talked about got me thinking. I'm curious if there's any evidence for them, or is it just her experience?"

"Evidence?" said Pete, with a raised eyebrow and a smirk.

"Okay. Research. You know, all those articles you and Rick get all worked up about," answered Melissa.

"So far, I'm seeing a lot—to confirm what she was saying."

"Such as?" inquired Pete.

"I started with gratitude. Maybe it's the time of year, but I see how important it can be year-round. I know you and Rick always define things first, so I found one for you."

Gratitude is a mindful awareness of the benefits in one's life.[2]

"I've seen so many articles on why I should start a gratitude journal, and I skim them over. But now I think maybe I should start one," said Melissa.

Focusing on gratitude is a wise move. Gratitude has been

found to increase positive emotions, decrease negative ones, and reduce dysfunctional behaviors.[3] Scientific evidence shows it's associated with enhanced psychological and physical well-being.[4] It helps relieve stress and reduces frustration. It also keeps you away from social comparison, which leads to toxic emotions such as envy and regret.[5] It's also been found to reduce "materialistic strivings" by helping you focus more attention on the gifts you already have.[6]

Gratitude isn't just a private, solo kind of exercise. It turns your attention beyond yourself to the well-being of other people. Glenn Fox, a neuroscientist at USC, found brain regions associated with interpersonal bonding correlated with feelings of gratitude in a brain imaging study.[7] It's a skill you can practice and get better at gradually.[8]

"I guess the most important thing is to begin. I see research supporting different ways to do this. Some of the specific practices I'm reading about look interesting. I need to look into them a bit more," said Melissa. "For now, let's just be grateful for each other and enjoy the rest of the ride home."

The following Saturday, when Pete came downstairs, Melissa was already in their home office. "Remember you asked how we can get more gratitude in our lives?" she said after he kissed her good morning.

"I'm all ears," answered Pete.

"There's a practice I like that's called Three Blessings.[9] It's straightforward. Simply reflect on three gifts you feel grateful for in your life," she said.

"Like counting your blessings?" asked Pete.

"Sort of. But it's more powerful."

Many things about gratitude are counterintuitive. First, it is not necessarily something you have to do every day. Research shows journaling two times a week raises well-being more than if you do it every day. Reflecting on your challenges and failures, along with your successes, will lead to more gratitude than if you only concentrate on successes alone.[10] And thinking about the things you treasure produces more gratitude if you imagine their *absence* from your life rather than their presence.

"I was surprised to see so many other effective gratitude practices," said Melissa. "Two, in particular, stood out to me: gratitude letters and visits. They benefit both the sender and the receiver, but especially the sender."

The practice involves making a list of the people who've had a positive impact on your life and writing handwritten letters thanking them for the difference they've made.[11] Research showed presenting gratitude letters in person had a more lasting effect on happiness, especially if you read it out loud as a testimonial."[12]

"Okay. I'll try it," said Pete.

"Remember how Aunt Al also talked about joy?" Melissa continued.

"Sure," said Pete, "when she contrasted adults and children."

"There's a growing body of studies on gratitude. But joy is the least researched of all the positive emotions, even though it's important,"[13] Melissa said.

She offered a definition:

Joy is the emotion evoked by well-being, success, or good fortune, or by the prospect of possessing what one desires, the expression or exhibition of such emotion, a state of happiness or felicity, and a source or cause of delight.[14]

"Sign me up for more of that," Pete said.

"Think of joy as a reaction to something good happening or something you're anticipating coming to fruition. Much like gratitude, it's relational. It connects us with other people. Joy is related to gratitude, but it's separate and distinct. They reinforce each other. The more gratitude you experience, the more likely you are to feel more joy. And vice versa."[15]

"So, how do we bring more joy to our lives? Where do we start?" wondered Pete.

"An audit," replied Melissa.

"Audit?" said Pete. "What happened to *delight*?"

"A joy audit.[16] We look at the different areas of our lives, where we experience it today and where we don't but would like to. Just doing this audit will help us be more aware of the opportunities for joy that are all around us," explained Melissa.

"I can do that," replied Pete.

"Let's do that separately, then compare notes."

"Deal," answered Pete.

"And there's one more step we can try. We can be more mindful about our physical surroundings so that they can lead to more joy," added Melissa.

"You mean like in the Marie Kondo book *The Life-Changing Magic of Tidying Up* you gave me?" Pete said.

"The one you ironically *lost* and couldn't find in your cluttered home office?" Melissa answered.

"I was afraid you'd put me in the *Doesn't Spark Joy* pile," said Pete.

"Don't be silly. I think we should do it together now so when we move to the city, we can start fresh," said Melissa.

In her book *Joyful*, Ingrid Fetell Lee, a former Design Director at IDEO, highlighted small changes that can make a big difference. One is to make a list of *Killjoys*—the things that diminish joy.[17] There are certain places, tasks, and objects that can drain your joy and energy. Listing them is a good first step toward finding ways to have less of them in your life. And sometimes all it takes is a tweak. Maybe you love to cook but hate to do the clean-up. Adding the right music can shift how you experience that task.

Melissa continued her research recap, next diving into Aunt Al's third point: the importance of humor.

Studies show humor is an effective way to relieve stress, tension, and anxiety.[18] Humor is associated with mental health, but it depends on the type of humor. But there are different styles. A meta-analysis of thirty-seven studies found some kinds of humor promote good health while others do not. For example, affiliative kinds of humor help grease the skids in social interactions and interpersonal relationships[19] whereas there's a negative correlation between self-deprecating humor and overall mental health. The right kind of humor can strengthen resiliency and increase creative thinking and problem-solving.[20]

Not surprisingly, children laugh much more than adults.[21] Humor, gratitude, and joy are interconnected. Humor makes us more open to other positive emotions like joy.[22]

"So, we've agreed to try four new things: the joy audit, Marie Kondo's approach, the killjoy list, and the gratitude letters," summarized Melissa.

"Thanks for the scouting report," Pete said. "This is the best one yet."

As Pete took Bailey on their walk the next afternoon, he thought about what Aunt Al shared and Melissa had found.

Something was gnawing at him—he felt like he was forgetting something important.

As they walked through town past the high school, he noticed a door propped open to the gym. He heard the familiar sounds: the bounce of the basketball, the squeak of the sneakers, the whistle, the unmistakable sound of the ball swishing through the net.

Then it hit him. *Find what you love to do*—even if you have to look back to rediscover it.

TAKEAWAYS

1. Notice what gives you joy. Savor the big moments and the surprising moments, but don't overlook small moments of joy. They're all around you in your daily life if you look for them.
2. Learn what takes away your joy and address it.
3. Practice gratitude. Find a regular way to appreciate what you have. You can start by building a new habit for it.
4. Look for positive humor. Drop any snarky, mean-spirited, sarcastic, or passive-aggressive humor you may have picked up in your working years. Office environments can be full of those types of humor, and you'll be surprised how much of that you may have picked up. Redirect yours to be self-deprecating. If you're like me, you'll find plenty of material there.

Try one or more of the exercises Pete and Melissa are experimenting with. They are simple, but powerful.

EXERCISES—BRING MORE GRATITUDE & JOY TO RETIREMENT

You can find more information on the exercises here:

Start a Gratitude Journal:

https://positivepsychology.com/gratitude-apps/

Write a Gratitude Letter:

https://positivepsychology.com/wp-content/uploads/
Gratitude-Letter1.pdf

Do a Gratitude Visit:

https://ggia.berkeley.edu/practice/practice_as_pdf/
gratitude_letter?printPractice

Do a Joy Audit:

https://www.theguardian.com/lifeandstyle/2020/jan/01/
how-to-have-more-fun-in-2020

Create a Killjoy List:

https://goop.com/wellness/mindfulness/
how-to-rediscover-joy/

CHAPTER ELEVEN

UNLOCK A NEW PURPOSE TO ELIMINATE DRIFT

"You get to a place where you begin to be guided by something greater than yourself. You stop fighting and striving and instead surrender to your higher purpose and be guided from there, allowing things to happen, focusing on your why and letting go of the how."[1]

—DR. WAYNE DYER

Melissa was surprised to see Pete up so early on a Saturday morning. She noticed he had already finished breakfast and was doing something out on the patio. "Good morning, dear! You're up early," she said.

Pete was feverishly working an air pump to reflate a dusty, well-worn basketball. "Good morning," Pete replied. "Bailey and I are off to the park to shoot some hoops."

Melissa frowned. "It's been a long time since you played. Be careful."

"No need to worry," Pete said." I'm not playing. Just shooting around for fun."

The court at the park was empty. Pete loved the feel of the ball in his hands. *It's been a while*, he thought as he took his first shot, mindful of his form and follow-through. *Clang!* Bailey looked away as the ball caromed violently off the metal backboard. *Oh well. It's time to go back to my old practice routine*, Pete thought.

As a young high school player, Pete had a chance encounter early one morning with an NBA Hall of Famer. Pete asked him how he learned to shoot so well. The player, the late Sam Jones of the Boston Celtics, didn't answer the question. Instead, he took the ball from Pete. He stood five feet away from the basket and banked in five shots in a row. He then moved back another five feet and banked in ten without a miss. He moved back again and hit fifteen in a row. He smiled at Pete, flipped him the ball, and walked away. The lesson that practice pays off always stuck with Pete. *Maybe practicing will help with retirement*, he mused.

Pete was rusty, but his old routine re-established his rhythm. He hit his last five shots in a row from the top of the key. "I think that's a good note to end on for today," he said to Bailey.

A group of players had gathered, shooting around at the other end of the court. A tall man who appeared to be in his early sixties approached Pete. "Good shooting, young man. Hi. I'm Sean. I haven't seen you here before."

"I haven't been over here for years. Just came back to shoot around a bit," answered Pete.

"We have a group of guys that meet here every Saturday morning at 10:00 and Wednesdays at 6:00. This time of year, we play half-court. We're short one player this morning. Will you join us so we can play three-on-three?" asked Sean.

"I'd love to, but I haven't played in years. It wouldn't be pretty," replied Pete. "Maybe in a few weeks when I get my wind back."

There was something in Sean's look that made Pete change his mind. "Okay, maybe one game."

Sean smiled broadly. "Once you come back to basketball, it's hard to stay away."

One game became three. After an hour, Pete knew he needed to call it quits. But it was great to play again. He didn't shoot much but concentrated instead on passing and defense. The movements came back more quickly than he expected. The competition was refreshing. Luckily, he had kept up his daily workout habit after taking Bailey on their morning walk. He was in good shape, but he quickly realized he wasn't in *basketball* shape.

"See you on Wednesday at 6:00?" Sean asked as Pete collected Bailey for the walk home.

Pete hesitated but answered, "If I can still walk, I will be here."

CELEBRATION

On Tuesday afternoon, Pete entered the restaurant downtown, wincing. After his return to basketball the previous weekend, he was still hurting in places he forgot he had. Seated at a table in the back, Matt spied him and waved him over.

"Thanks for coming," said Matt warmly. "It's great to see you!"

"Thanks for the invite. It's great to catch up," said Pete. "How are things going?"

"I have big news. I got the funding! Sarah, the angel investor we met with in New York, came through 100 percent!" said Matt.

"That's terrific!" replied Pete. "I'm so happy for you!"

"It's thanks to you. It was your help that made the difference," said Matt.

"So, this is a celebration lunch," added Pete.

"Mostly. I wanted to say thank you, but it's a business lunch, too. I have an idea to discuss," Matt said.

"Celebration first," replied Pete. "So, tell me all about it. When did you find out?" he asked.

"Two weeks ago. Sarah and her team called, and we went through everything in detail. Ever since then, it's been lawyers 24/7 finalizing everything," Matt said.

"How do you feel?" asked Pete.

"I feel great, but it's a little overwhelming. Sarah has high expectations and aggressive timeframes. There's a lot to get done," Matt said. "I have more than enough funding to build out my team, and I want to get that right."

"That's important. What's your plan?" asked Pete.

"Well, that's what I wanted to discuss. I have a former colleague lined up to become the CFO and COO. And I'd like to recruit you to become our Head of Strategy and Planning. Sarah's totally on board with it," said Matt.

"Matt, I'm flattered, but I decided earlier this year to take early retirement. I'm done with corporate life. So, thank you, but I'm out of the game," said Pete.

"I hear you," replied Matt. "But this is different. It's a venture-backed start-up. I can use your experience and advice, and I think you'll find the start-up environment rejuvenating."

"Well, I'm pretty rejuvenated. Thanks though. I sincerely appreciate the offer," said Pete.

"That's the thing—you haven't *seen* the offer yet," Matt said as he handed Pete an envelope. "I think it may change your mind. It includes an equity stake. I should tell you that Sarah pushed me to increase the stake. We both think you're critical for the launch."

Pete was speechless for a moment. "Okay. Let me think about it. When do you need an answer?"

"I was hoping for today. But take your time. I'm meeting with Sarah next in two weeks. I'll need to know by then."

Pete was making progress on Melissa's commitment to be more helpful around the house, although there were still miles to go. One thing he was consistent about was making dinner most nights during the week. His cooking range was gradually expanding. Tonight, he was finishing his signature vegan stir-fry dish when Melissa returned from work.

As they caught up on how their days had gone, Melissa asked how his lunch with Matt went.

"Great news!" answered Pete. "He got the funding. He's building out his team. He's pumped. I'm so happy for him."

"That's great. But what are the company's prospects? Do you think it'll make it?" asked Melissa.

"Hard to say. The failure rate is so high. But now Matt's backed by a deep-pocketed savvy investor who's well-connected. That should definitely help him," Pete said before pausing.

"He also made me an offer to join him," he added.

"Well, you always talked about how sharp he is," said Melissa with a smile.

Pete explained the details, and Melissa, ever the lawyer, asked if he wanted her to review the documents.

Later that night, Melissa circled back. "This is an attractive offer. How did you respond?"

"I told him no. But then I agreed to think about it," Pete said.

"I know you'll make the right call," Melissa said. "But if you want to talk it over, let me know when you're ready. If this thing hits, it could be a sizable payday."

"I know," said Pete.

Pete was becoming a regular at the Wednesday and Saturday games at the park. Most of the other players were around the same age and ability level as Pete. Sean was the oldest, the tallest, and by far the most skillful player. Pete noticed Sean seemed to play at half-speed most of the time except when a game was on the line, when he would flash the full power of his game. Then his moves were swift, precise, and deadly.

In between games, Pete struck up a conversation with Sean. "How long have you been playing here?" Pete asked.

"About four years," Sean replied. "I can see you also know your way around a basketball court. Where did you used to play?"

"I played on a good high school team. Back then, it was all I thought or cared about," said Pete with a laugh. "How about you? Where did you play ball? College?"

"I played at a small college down South. And I had a cup of coffee in the pros," said Sean.

"It shows," said Pete.

"Hey, now that it's getting colder, we move our game indoors. Same days, same times. More players, and we go full-court. You in?" asked Sean.

"I don't know if I'm ready to go full-court yet," said Pete.

"Well, I can ease you into it," said Sean. "See you Saturday at 10:00?"

Pete hesitated but said, "Okay. I'm in. Where's the gym?"

After getting Sean's full name from one of the other players, Pete did a little research on his playing career. While he wasn't a star, he had more than a cup of coffee in the pros. Following college was a second-round pick in the NBA draft, and he played in the ABA for two years and three seasons in the NBA, including a trip to NBA Finals, before finishing up with a season in Europe.[2]

Looks like there's more than meets the eye with Sean, thought Pete.

SCOUTING REPORT: PURPOSE VERSUS DRIFT

Pete had mixed feelings as he approached Rick's office for their last meeting. Pete liked to say he "didn't do sad." But he was a bit sad today. Pete realized he'd miss their meetings. He also wondered if he was fully ready to "graduate," as Melissa called it. And he was curious about the topic of the last scouting report.

GRADUATION DAY?

Rick greeted Pete warmly as he entered his office. His finger, broken from basketball several weeks earlier, had healed and Pete was impressed with how firm his handshake was already. They spent a few minutes catching up on what had happened since they last met. He shared his takeaways from their visit with Aunt Al. "It's still early days, but I think Melissa and I are both getting a lot out of the gratitude exercises we're both doing. It helps me notice and appreciate more.

"And remember the entrepreneur I was helping? Matt? He received the full funding he was seeking."

"Great news," replied Rick, "It sounds like you helped him quite a bit."

"I just helped him see a few of his blind spots. Awareness goes a long way," said Pete. "I'm just happy for him. It's a great opportunity."

"You're probably wondering why I kept this last scouting report a mystery," said Rick. "I find that if someone isn't ready for it, it can seem overwhelming. If you think back to where we started, you've come a long way. Now, you've reached the highest level of the Retirement Game. You have the chance to unlock the path to a truly satisfying life in retirement. It's the final battle, and you're ready for it. It differentiates a great retirement from a good one, but it's the hardest to achieve.

"The last challenge you'll face is cultivating a new sense of purpose," Rick said.

"Is a new purpose something everyone finds in retirement?" asked Pete.

"No," answered Rick. "That's why I call this the championship round. Many people don't do it, but it is achievable."

A study by Stanford University and Encore.org of 1,200 adults age fifty and over found 31 percent reported a sense of purpose beyond themselves. It did not vary across demographic factors like age, income, health, or location. They found some interesting differences between those who reported having a purpose and those who did not. One is positivity, with 94 percent of the purpose group indicating a positive outlook on life.[3]

"I see clear options emerging for me, but it sounds overwhelming to think about finding a new purpose," said Pete.

"An alternative word that resonates more with some people is mission. If you were on a new mission, what would it be?" replied Rick.

"That's helpful. I'll give it some thought. How do you define purpose, Rick?" asked Pete.

"I like this definition," said Rick.

> Purpose is a self-organizing life aim that stimulates goals, promotes healthy behaviors, and gives meaning to life.[4]

There are four parts to purpose, and each one leads to the next:

1. A self-organizing life aim
2. Clear goals
3. Healthy behaviors
4. Meaning

"The phrase self-organizing jumps out at me. Why is that important?" asked Pete.

"It's important to have a new driving force in your life. It will help guide you on how you'll structure your days and spend your time," answered Rick. "We've talked about the paradox of retirement. It gives you the freedom you may have been longing for, but it's completely up to you to decide how you'll use it. Some people find it liberating; many find it paralyzing."

"It sounds like I just met our opponent in this round," said Pete.

"Yes," said Rick. "Drift is the downside of the freedom of retirement. Just like a leaf floating along a stream, when you're drifting in retirement, you're not in control of the direction you're heading in. And while the ride may be pleasant, you might not like where you end up. You've experienced this. You go from a structured, dynamic environment with forces pressing on you to a life with lesser demands. It's nice to live without the structure for a while, but it can be unsatisfying. For a lot of us, our purpose has been defined primarily by work, partially because that's where we have spent most of our time."

Researchers estimate most adults will spend 90,000 hours working over their lifetimes.[5]

A study by the Rand Corporation found that 80 percent of workers in the US reported deriving meaning from their job always or most of the time. That number was highest among older college-educated men.[6]

Exiting work can leave a giant hole. If you loved your work, you're likely feeling a loss of your professional identity. You'll find yourself wondering, *Who am I now?* Purpose is missing, but even in retirement, work—in whatever form you choose—can become a source of purpose again. Forty percent of workers sixty-five and over had retired at some point before deciding to *unretire.* Almost half of the overall retirees surveyed (and 57 percent of those who were college-educated) said they would return to work for the right opportunity.[7]

Drift leads people away from finding a new purpose. Sadly, the *average* retiree ends up watching forty-eight hours of television each week, according to Nielsen audience data (and that was before the pandemic).[8]

A survey by the Stanford Center on Longevity asked baby boomers what they expected to be doing at age sixty-five. While most expect to be enjoying retirement, 18 percent expect to be still working, 22 percent anticipate working but not as much, and 13 percent expect to be working but doing something new and different.[9]

PURPOSE AND HEALTH

"I'm surprised to see *healthy behaviors* in the definition," Pete said. "I hadn't thought of purpose like that."

"It's one of the reasons why purpose is so important in retirement," said Rick.

There's a growing body of research indicating that leading a purposeful life may have significant health benefits.[10] For one, it can help you stay sharp. Studies by Patricia Boyle at The University of Chicago have suggested people who report a strong sense of purpose have a 30 percent slower rate of cognitive decline.[11] Having a sense that your life has purpose has been found to support the health of the central nervous system and to increase resilience in dealing with adversity.[12]

Purpose leads people to be more engaged in activities promoting physical and mental health, contributing to a better overall quality of life. It's linked to higher levels of physical activity, involvement with community-oriented goals,[13] and higher levels of social engagement.[14] A study from the University of Michigan of over 7,000 people fifty-plus found a stronger purpose was associated with decreased rates of mortality.[15]

GOALS...IN RETIREMENT?

"Some people get stuck on purpose as a lofty concept," said Rick. "But goals translate inspiring visions into tangible actions. They bring aspirations into reality.

"And you need more than goals," he continued. "You can fall into the trap of just focusing on the tangible short-term goals and taking steps toward them."

Without an inspiring, broader vision of purpose, activities can end up feeling hollow and, ultimately, dissatisfying. You need a compelling *Why*. It's about more than merely keeping busy. One scholar observed that retirees who were diligent workers need outlets for their productive energy, but in meaningful pursuits. He warned that just staying busy with unmeaningful activities is a symptom of avoidance.[16] Researchers have found that the driving force of purpose mitigates the challenges of the transition to retirement and boosts well-being.[17] Just the process of simply setting goals for your retirement life is ultimately more important than the nature of the goals themselves. Setting goals creates a sense of direction that can ease the transition.[18]

A study of retirees in the UK found that an upfront investment in self-reflection enhanced goal setting.[19] It pays to take the time to think about what really matters to you now. Things that were priorities in your full-time career years may not be top-of-mind going forward. Start by examining the things that energize you, both at work and outside of work,[20] and note what things give you the most meaning.

Harry Kraemer, Professor at Northwestern's Kellogg School of Management, former CEO of Baxter International, and author of *Your 168: Finding Purpose and Satisfaction in a Values-Based Life,* points out that how you invest your time is the litmus test for what really matters to you. Think of it this way: if someone filmed your life for a week like a reality TV show, what would they assume about your values based on your choices?

When it comes to pursuing activities that align with your values, it helps to have someone who can help hold you accountable. Kraemer recommends having people in your life who will call you out when your actions are out of sync with your values. It could be a sibling; it could be a colleague or your old roommate. Whoever it is, they have to be able to say, "I hear you talking about your values, but I'm looking at your actions, and the words and the music aren't working together."[21]

WHAT GIVES MEANING TO YOUR LIFE NOW?

Purpose is all about meaning, but what's meaningful to you may not be meaningful to someone else. Furthermore, everyone lives a new purpose in different ways. A study of people sixty-five and older found that retirees are setting goals in multiple life areas, including wellness, personal growth, and learning new skills. The most common focus is on relationship goals, which older adults find most personally meaningful. Volunteering and service are also significant areas for goal setting. Retirees actively involved in volunteer activities report a stronger sense of purpose, happiness, and self-esteem.[22]

Such activities also can have positive impacts on health. Volunteers have a lower risk of hypertension, delayed onset of physical disability, and enhanced cognition. A study indicated 29 percent of baby boomers expect to volunteer in retirement.[23]

Purpose is powered by a desire to do something for others beyond yourself, to contribute to the greater good in a meaningful way. The late Wayne Dyer described it as moving from success to significance.[24]

As he often was, Rick was ready with an example.

PROFILE: DR. CYNTHIA BARNETT

Dr. Cynthia Barnett is living proof that when one door closes, another opens. When her career in education abruptly ended, Barnett created a new avenue for teaching. Inspired by a research study highlighting the relative absence of women in STEM (science, technology, engineering, and math), she built The Amazing Girls Science Program.[25]

The program encourages girls to explore STEM subjects while also teaching them critical life skills, such as self-confidence, creative problem-solving, curiosity, prudent risk-taking, and resilience. Barnett was awarded the Inaugural AARP Purpose Prize for her work.

In the face of adversity, she chose resilience and perseverance. "I made a decision that I was going to swim, and I was not going to sink. And one of the things I learned from that difficult situation and that really bubbled up in me was my own problem-solving skills. I learned how to figure it out. I had an inner strength in me that I didn't know existed. I learned how to be independent and how to be confident. And it was a challenging time, but I made it through."

She credits self-reflection as a critical factor. "Sometimes, it's difficult. It depends on the mindset where one may be thinking about how they want to lead their life. It's a lot about reflection. And thinking, *Well, now it's time. It's time to do something else. It's time to give back. It's time to truly make a difference.*"

Barnett encourages people to tune in to their inner voice for guidance and direction. "That inner calling, it just speaks to us if people are really willing to think of where they're going next, where they want to spend the next twenty years—because research shows that we are going to live to another twenty or thirty years after we leave the regular workforce. I left my position as an assistant high school principal seventeen years ago. I was sixty at the time. I'm going to be seventy-seven next month. And I'm thinking, *What would I have done in all that time?* I would have been absolutely bored. It's so important to really think of what's next for us, and many people don't think about that."

MENTORING

The pandemic highlighted the value of intergenerational relationships and mentoring. It's a way for experienced people to pass along their knowledge and wisdom to the next generations.

"Of all the things I've done, mentoring is the one thing I especially like to do," Pete told Rick. "I'm motivated by it, and if I can say so, I'm pretty good at it."

"The people you're mentoring sure seem to think so," said Rick.

Mentoring offers a good fit between supply and demand. One study noted that 50 percent of people fifty and older in the US want to be mentors, and more than half of people under fifty are interested in being mentored, with two-thirds of Gen Z wanting mentors.[26] Best of all? True mentoring isn't one-directional. Both parties learn from each other. It's mutually beneficial.

"All of this makes me think about the scouting report we did about callings. I have a much better picture of my options now. But I wouldn't say I have a calling. What's the difference between a calling and a new purpose?" asked Pete.

"Great question," answered Rick. "They're related, but a calling tends to become a singular focus. Some people get stuck looking for a single purpose. Most people's lives are multidimensional. When they retire from their primary career, that doesn't change. Most feel a need to replace the central purpose work provided, but not necessarily with one thing. Think of it as creating a *portfolio* of interests. You can decide which are primary and secondary, and you can set goals in each area."

"It's like our investment portfolio, only about my time. Both are diversified," added Pete.

"Exactly," said Rick.

"But how can you have time for *multiple purposes*? That sounds stressful," said Pete. "How can I get my arms around my new purpose or purposes?"

"There are a few short exercises that can help make purpose feel more real. I'll email them to you," said Rick.

"More homework?" protested Pete with a laugh. "I thought I was graduating today! Now you're making me find my purpose?"

"You don't need to find your purpose to graduate, Pete,"

answered Rick. You already have it. You just need to unlock it and start living it. And I'll bet you'll discover more than one."

Rick summarized the exercises. The first will ask Pete to make a list of his values and what's most important to him right now. The second one, borrowed from Stephen Covey, author of *The 7 Habits of Highly Effective People*,[27] will ask him to write a personal mission statement in just one to four paragraphs. The last will ask him to look at the different roles he has in his life and list his goals for each. Rick explained he could do the exercises in any order as long as he did them all.

Pete suspected there was more to it.

"I should know better by now, but I'll ask anyway. I heard you say it's a series of exercises. What else?" asked Pete.

"Indeed. It's a reality check," replied Rick. "Look at your calendar for the last month. Take an objective look at how you're allocating your time. Work with the list of values you created and rank them in order of their importance to you. Then estimate the amount of time you're currently spending on each one. Finally, identify the changes you want to make going forward to invest your time more in line with your values."

"I can see how this makes purpose real," said Pete. "I feel like we need another meeting."

"Take your time and do those exercises, then get started with *living* your purpose," Rick said. "Any time you want to meet after that, just let me know. The exercises will help you clarify some things. But keep taking action. It's the best way to learn."

"Okay. But what should I start *doing*?" asked Pete.

"Keep your eyes open for opportunities," answered Rick. "Trust yourself, Pete. You'll know when it's right."

THE PURPOSE WORKOUT

Pete jumped into the exercises. Rick recommended he take his time with them, but Pete felt a sense of urgency. He thought they could help him sharpen his thinking about Matt's offer. The exercises pulled him toward a sense that there were things he could do to make a difference beyond jumping back into the world of full-time work. But what exactly?

He was still leaning *no* on Matt's offer. But Melissa kept hinting at what they could do with the financial windfall if Matt's company took off in a few years. Maybe Aunt Al was right. Perhaps he was too young to retire after all. Pete was feeling more torn than he expected.

THE GYM OF LIFE

The gym where Sean's group played in the winter was downtown, in an unfamiliar part of the city. Pete allowed for extra time when he headed there on Saturday. He arrived twenty minutes early and went inside. There was a lot of noise coming from the gym. He wasn't sure what he had expected, but the dilapidated space had certainly seen better days.

Sean was holding court with a group of about twenty players. It wasn't the guys Pete played with, but a far younger group. They looked to be in their mid-teens. They were listening to Sean intently. When he blew a whistle, the group quickly disbanded and headed off in four sub-groups to do a series of drills. Ten minutes later, the whistle blew again, and the players hustled to center court. Sean complimented them on how precisely they had executed the drills. He shifted gears and started talking about the importance of building the proper habits in the right way. Sean was teaching them how to develop laser-focus by practicing the same things over and over with keen attention to detail. Without that level of focus, Sean believed you could get good at doing something the wrong way. He closed with a quote from Stephen Covey. "If you remember one thing from this morning, remember this: 'Your character is a composite of your habits.'"[28]

The teens left, and the other adults who had trickled in during the drills took the court to warm up. As Sean had mentioned, there were additional players for the full-court game. Sean gave Pete a brief rundown on each one. "That's Nick. He's a lawyer in his day job, and sadly, he argues every call here, too. That's Jim. He never met a shot he didn't like. If you pass the ball to him, you'll never see it again. It's going up. Guaranteed. And according to Nick, he fouls out within ten minutes each time we play."

A taller man walked in. "There's the smartest player here, Joey. Every game is a battle of strategy with him. He thinks two steps ahead of everyone."

"Good to know," said Pete. "I only count nine players. Are we one player short? I'll sit out."

"Hold on," said Sean. "We have one player who always arrives last. I guess he likes to make a dramatic entrance. He's the most intense competitor we have here. A sharpshooter. He doesn't look like much, but trust me, he's an assassin on the court."

The door opened, and an average-sized man in a hooded sweatshirt strolled in. "Ah. Here he is. C'mon. Let me introduce you. You'll want to get on his good side."

"Um. Thanks, Sean. No need." said Pete. "*Rick?*"

Sean's description of Rick on the court proved to be accurate. It was interesting to see Rick in action. And while Rick was the last to arrive, he was also the first to leave.

After Rick departed, Pete approached Sean. "I didn't know you coached youth basketball," he said.

"Well, it's more than that. I've built a program," answered Sean. "It's about teaching them what they'll need to know to make it out of here and succeed at something someday. I'm just using basketball, which they're already interested in, to teach them what I know about life. Hopefully, I'm planting some seeds for their future. It's the most important work I've ever done. If you have time on Wednesday, come by at 4:30. You can see what we do."

Pete had a lot to ponder on his way home. Monday was his deadline to give Matt an answer.

TAKEAWAYS

1. Don't get stuck on the idea of finding a singular new purpose. Many people discover multiple purposes that evolve from the various roles in retirement, including new ones.
2. Having a strong sense of purpose has multiple benefits for your physical and mental health, as well as your longevity and satisfaction.
3. Staying busy is unlikely to be satisfying to you in retirement unless you're involved in activities you find meaningful.
4. Self-reflection can help clarify your values and priorities at this stage of life. Your calendar is the evidence of what your priorities really are.

EXERCISES—FIND NEW PURPOSES

Will a multipurpose retirement be right for you? Invest some time to assess what matters most to you now and what possibilities you'll want to explore:

1. List your core values. Dig a bit deeper than the things you may usually cite. Challenge yourself to list five specific things that matter most to you now. Ensure you're mindful of things that may have been central in your full-time career years (like status and advancement) that may be less important to you going forward.
2. Look at how you've spent your time in the past month. How well does it align with the list of your core values?
3. Note the purposes you see in the different roles in your life. Which ones are the most important to you today?
4. Write a list of opportunities you see to experiment with activities that help others and contribute to the greater

good. Explore volunteering, mentoring, or part-time work opportunities that offer multigenerational interaction.

5. Draft a one-paragraph mission statement for your unique retirement that reflects what your new purpose(s) could become.

EPILOGUE

Bailey was sporting a new shamrock green collar on their early morning walk in the park. As they came in from the cold, the elevator door opened before Pete could punch the up button. To his surprise, Melissa was standing there. "I've got to run, dear. Another early meeting today," she said, petting Bailey and kissing Pete. "But I'll see you there at noon! Have a great day, CMO! It's a big day!" she said with a wave.

Yup, that's me—CMO, thought Pete. As he pressed the button for their floor, he smiled at Melissa's glee in teasing him with his new title. He glanced at his phone and quickly calculated how much time he had to get ready. He had his yoga class with Rebecca in her studio at 8:00, a meeting with Matt and his leadership team at 10:00, and the big event at noon, followed by lunch with Rick. Then his time was free until date night with Melissa. Two years earlier, she had received the big promotion she was after, and now Pete was even more concerned about her workload and long hours.

As he entered their apartment, Pete shook his head and chuckled about how much his life had changed. Today was the third anniversary of the day he was downsized over the phone by Mega Corp, a day that seemed like a lifetime ago. It had been two years since Matt's offer. And it was a year already since he and Melissa had moved to the city. He stopped for a minute and took in the view. It hadn't gotten old yet. He didn't think it ever would.

A BASKETBALL JONES

Two and a half years earlier, he had returned to playing basketball with Sean's group at the gym downtown. Over time, he got his game back. Basketball had helped him get back into shape, the best he'd been in years. But it had also given him something he hadn't expected—a community. The diverse group of players included executives, a doctor, a CPA, several government workers (including one whose job was shrouded in secrecy), a few local small business owners, a priest, a rabbi, a professor, and two lawyers. And Rick.

The games were intensely competitive, but friendships evolved off the court. Sean had started a tradition, and the group would gather at a nearby pub each Wednesday night after playing. There was always a degree of spirited trash-talking about the games they just played. Sometimes, the heated arguments about foul calls continued at the pub. But the group also celebrated significant life events: graduations, several weddings, and occasionally professional milestones. They also provided support through the illnesses and losses that inevitably occurred from time to time.

Pete had begun to come to more of the training sessions Sean was conducting for various age groups. Occasionally, Sean asked him to help with a drill or offer comments on his teaching. On the court, Pete was thriving. He especially enjoyed the cerebral aspects of the game. He took as much pleasure from anticipating a player's tendencies and making a great defensive play as he did hitting a game-winning shot. Pete was having fun.

Pete had also developed a friendly on-court rivalry with Rick. He looked forward to the times they were matched up against each other. Pete became obsessed with blocking Rick's shot, which was elusive because of his quick release. But one day, as Rick drove the baseline and headed to the hoop, Pete sensed an opportunity. Pete accelerated and elevated at just the right time, blocking Rick's shot against the backboard. As soon as he landed, he felt the pop. It was his left knee. He crumbled to the ground in pain as his friends quickly surrounded him. Neil, the doctor, took one look at the knee and immediately called an ambulance.

Pete's surgery went well, but the damage had been extensive. He wouldn't be playing basketball again for a while, if ever. The hardest part was going from being in great shape to being physically restricted. Pete was disappointed he couldn't play. He was down. But he was hopeful he could play again someday, and he threw himself into his rehab. His physical therapy, three times a week for six months, helped him regain stability and strength in and around the knee.

One day his physical therapist, Barbara, asked if he's ever done yoga. He explained that he had, but his yoga instructor had moved. She recommended her niece, who held classes downtown close to their apartment. "She's special. You'll see. It will help you. Give it a try," Barbara said.

Barbara was right. Yoga helped enormously. It was challenging, especially at first, but over time, Pete felt more comfortable with the poses. He saw how it aided his rehab. He was surprised, however, to see how Rebecca's practice taught him many things beyond the physical benefits of yoga, including mindfulness, calm, and gratitude.

Every once in a while, after his class, Pete would drop by the gym. He liked seeing everyone. He'd never tell them, but he missed them as much as he missed playing. Well, almost.

Sean was always happy to see Pete. He shared stories about various injuries he'd suffered in his playing career and tips on making the most of the rehab period. "One of the biggest benefits is it gives you time to reflect and think. Something good will come from it. You'll see," Sean said.

Sean asked Pete to stop by the gym when he could to share stories from his corporate career and what he had learned from them. While they were off the cuff at first, Pete began to prepare more for them. As his wheels started to turn, he began suggesting ideas for topics to cover.

Months later, Sean and Pete had collaborated and expanded the youth program. Keeping basketball at the center, they developed a series of three workshops for the high school players. They called them the three pillars.

The first one was on emotional intelligence. They started with how EQ could help their performance on the court, in school, and someday, in their work lives. Spurred by his work with Matt, Pete wanted to start training them early on the interpersonal skills they'd need to succeed. The next was about healthy habits covering how to get good nutrition and sleep right. The third was mental hygiene, covering optimism, resilience, mindfulness, and gratitude. In addition to Pete's and Sean's personal experiences, each workshop was supported by Pete's summary of relevant books he and Sean had read on the topic.

It took a while for the workshops to catch on. But once the teens saw how committed the two best players were, they wanted to be part of the workshops.

One day, Susan, the mother of one of the star players, approached Pete. She asked if she and a few other parents could attend the workshops. Pete hesitated at first, wondering if she had concerns about what they were teaching. Susan explained that she and other parents were so impressed with their kids' learning, they wanted to see how they could apply the material themselves. Pete and Sean agreed they could attend. "Why not?" said Sean. "These topics are useful at any age."

After a while, Pete realized it would help the high schoolers to hear some new voices. They agreed to invite a speaker once a month to talk about one of the pillars to test it out. Their first speaker was Dr. Cooper. His specialty was lifestyle medicine, and he spoke with the group about prevention and healthy habits they could begin right away. He shared his personal story of a medical wakeup call and the changes he made, including adopting a plant-based diet.

Unbeknownst to Pete, Susan had spread the word, and twenty-five parents from the community attended. Their second speaker was Rebecca, the owner of the yoga studio Pete attended. Her talk included getting the players and their parents to experience several basic yoga poses (which was a sight to behold) and a discussion of the benefits of yoga, including mindfulness and gratitude.

A major breakthrough came with their sixth speaker, Rob, a former teammate of Sean's. Rob had been a top NBA player and had gone on to become a popular broadcaster. He would be in town for an upcoming game and reached out to Sean to see if he was free for lunch. He was enthusiastic when Sean invited him to speak. When he arrived, the gym was packed— their players, friends, parents, and many people Pete had never seen piled in.

Rob's talk was on grit and perseverance. But he spent the first ten minutes regaling the crowd with hysterical stories about Sean back in the day. After he spoke, there was a line of people waiting to get his autograph. Sean teased Rob, asking him if he realized more people there knew him from his charismatic broadcasting career than his playing days. Rob ignored him and kept signing, but said, "Sean, I think you've got something special you're building here. But why are you holding this program in such a dump?"

Sean smiled and replied, "We don't all have your level of wealth, Rob. I've never been in your ZIP code, remember?"

Rob shook his head. "I'm not talking about you, knucklehead. There are other ways you can do this better. We should talk."

MATT'S COMPANY

As Pete took his seat at the table for the 10:00 meeting with Matt's leadership team, he was glad to see that Sarah, the angel investor, was attending as well.

After some deliberation, Pete had politely but firmly declined Matt's offer two years earlier. He was not going back to a full-time working life. But Matt, with Sarah's urging behind the scenes, wouldn't take no for an answer. Ultimately, they crafted a role that fit Pete's talents and his need for balance. He came on board with a monthly retainer as a part-time consultant, with a firm cap on the time he would spend working each month. At Sarah's suggestion, Matt included a pro-rated equity stake. With the new arrangement, Pete came on board as the CMO—chief *mentoring* officer.

His role initially concentrated on guiding Matt as he hired talent and marched toward a product launch. As the company grew, Pete's time was allocated for mentoring other key people in the company, in line with what Sarah had envisioned. It was impactful, and the company's growth was so rapid that Pete got the green light to hire a small team of full-time mentors/coaches. He recruited his old boss, Jim, who had volunteered with SCORE, and his protégé Joanna from his old company.

The morning's meeting was a big one. A larger company was interested in buying Matt's firm. Ruth, an investment banker, was briefing the team on the outlines of the deal. Pete was thrilled for Matt, but he couldn't keep his mind on track. He kept thinking about his next meeting at noon.

WHAT A DIFFERENCE THINKING BIG MAKES

A lot had happened since the day Sean's former teammate Rob spoke at the gym a year and a half earlier. It was a huge turning point. Now they were all there outside at a vacant lot downtown for the event at noon. There were far more people in attendance than Pete expected as he surveyed the scene. Sarah and Matt were seated in the front row with the city's NBA franchise owner. Sean was being interviewed by the famous TV personality reporter, Sloane Bassett, who was covering the event. He noticed Nick and Joey from the basketball gang, Joanna chatting with Rebecca, and James, the mayor. Barbara, his physical therapist, was talking with Michael and Caroline from Matt's company. Even Patricia, the woman who raised guide dogs for the blind who Pete interviewed, had come. And Rick was in the back row, taking it all in.

Melissa breezed in, with the head of her law firm. "I'm so proud of you, Pete," she said, taking her seat along with their son and daughter, who made the trip to surprise their dad.

They were all there for the ground-breaking ceremony for the new community center that Sean and Pete had come to envision. It would include a new gym, a fitness center, and meeting space for their workshops, which had expanded significantly. There would be a yoga studio where Rebecca and her team had agreed to offer classes for the community. They had enough funding to hire a dedicated staff and could now expand their program more broadly.

Their vision had become clear, but it had taken work. Pete sprang into action and worked to form a public-private partnership of potential backers. He leveraged all his contacts from both his old life and his new life. Sean and Rob secured commitments from the local NBA team. Once the NBA came on board, Melissa connected Pete with colleagues who made introductions to key people in city government. Sarah also came through again, bringing in a major Silicon Valley firm to secure the naming rights to the center and sponsor a technology training program to be offered there. Interviews with Sean's players and their parents in the local press on how the program had impacted them created a buzz about the project. Now they were breaking ground. It wasn't easy, but the vision was becoming a reality.

LESSONS LEARNED

Rick had invited Pete to lunch to celebrate following the ceremony. Apart from basketball, they hadn't met one-on-one in quite some time. To Pete's surprise, Rick had reserved a private room at Pete's favorite restaurant. The first thing Pete noticed was the champagne.

"Is this to celebrate the anniversary of the time I blocked your shot?" asked Pete, "*and* pinned it against the backboard?"

"Very funny," said Rick. "Let the record show you did *not* pin it against the backboard. I'm sorry to break it to you, but you couldn't jump that well back then. But really, congratulations. What you've pulled together is phenomenal."

"What a long, strange trip it's been," said Pete. "And none of it would have happened without our work together. So, thank you."

After they ordered, Rick said, "In addition to celebrating, I thought this might be a good occasion for us to have that final wrap-up conversation if you're up for it."

"Ah," said Pete, with an eye roll. "I should have known. But no scouting report, right?"

"No," said Rick with a laugh, "just a brief look back. I'm curious about what made the most difference for you. What was the most useful?"

"I can tell you right off the bat that doing all of those exercises mattered," said Pete. "They made me reflect, take action, and observe. The exercises led me to do some experiments, and that helped me most.

"The scouting reports prepared me well for the tensions and the battles that arose along the way. But learning from experience was the key. That helped me become more open-minded and weave my way forward."

"Which scouting reports stand out?" asked Rick.

"The first one struck me. When I first found myself outside the workplace, I was afraid I'd be bored. I missed the action from work. Looking back, I *was* a little bored after a while. But what you taught me about curiosity helped tremendously. It was an attitude adjustment that helped me to keep asking questions and investigating things, which was key," said Pete.

"Then, learning about change and self-efficacy and personal agency helped me take charge. Those scouting reports made me realize that whatever I did choose to do next was totally on me.

I needed to accept change and take the initiative to create a new path," said Pete. "I knew I wouldn't be happy with the status quo, but I also knew I had a lot of options. I had to own my future."

"Which challenges were the hardest for you?" asked Rick.

"Definitely uncertainty. I *craved* clarity. I was impatient living with a lack of direction. I felt adrift. I lived with that for quite a long time, until we got to purpose."

"What happened then?" asked Rick.

"When we talked about a *multipurpose retirement*, it clicked for me. I felt the pressure leave me right away. I thought, *I can do that*. Before then, I felt like I was failing early retirement. I felt like I should have a calling but must have a weak cell connection or something. I hadn't found that singular driving purpose. I felt like I was supposed to find that *One Big Thing*. But by then, I was used to picking up different things along the way, thanks to curiosity, and trying them out felt less risky," said Pete.

"To your credit, you were willing to try a lot of things along the way," said Rick.

"When I look back, they were small things, but they helped me explore and broaden my horizons," said Pete. "Playing the guitar again. Working out on the bike each morning after I came in with Bailey. Art class. Yoga," said Pete. "I even learned to cook...well, cook better at least.

"And looking back, I didn't go out in search of my new purpose. A few different purposes *found me* when I wasn't looking.

"When I think about it now, I could have blown off Jim when he asked me to help Matt with SCORE," Pete continued. "I could have easily avoided Joanna when she needed advice at my old company. I certainly could have stayed home and said no to helping out Sean when I was on crutches.

"But those small steps worked because I had become more open-minded, and I was more willing to try things. Funnily enough, social connectivity helped most," Pete said. "My new purposes all evolved from getting involved with people in those small moments, and they grew from there."

"It's funny you mentioned the role of uncertainty," said Rick. "There's emerging research that's in sync with your experience. It turns out uncertainty can sharpen our thinking. It shocks us out of complacency to find a new answer by trying more novel things.[1] Okay. End of scouting report. It's great to see the life you've built, Pete. Well done."

"Thanks. I feel like I've created a mix that's right for me, and I'm helping others. I've hit my stride again. But in some ways, I feel like I'm just getting started."

"I have one more question for you," added Pete.

"Sure," said Rick.

"*Now*, do I graduate?" asked Pete with a grin.

"Well, you said it yourself. You're just getting started," answered Rick. "Remember, learning is a lifetime sport."[2]

"I can live with that," said Pete. "It reminds me that learning isn't just research—it comes from doing new things, and it can be fun."

Pete continued, "Oh, I wanted to tell you that I completed art class, and I have one more gift for you."

It was Pete's third painting. The first two were self-portraits reflecting how Pete felt at those points in his transition to early retirement. Pete wasn't in the third. It captured a moment at one of Sean's "life lesson" workshops, with a group of players and some of their parents. It was titled *Paying It Forward.*

"I thought you'd appreciate this one," said Pete. "Thank *you.* But don't get carried away," he added. "My fourth one is titled *The Block: Sending It Back.* I'm working on getting the look on your face exactly right when I blocked your shot that day."

The best part of Pete's day was the last part: date night. Melissa suggested staying in and hanging out together by the fire after dinner. "And just talk," she said. "You know, like we used to."

They talked about the day's events and Pete's lunch with Rick.

"You're not really doing a painting called *The Block.* Are you?" said Melissa.

"No, but I should," said Rick. "You should have seen it."

"Stop right there. I've heard this story before—*many times,*" Melissa said. "Did you forget what happened when you landed? And the surgery and all those physical therapy sessions?

And when I had to help you put your socks on every day, for months? Shall I continue?"

"Okay. You got me," said Pete.

"But seriously, Pete. I'm so happy for you. You've come a long way," said Melissa. "And today really showed it."

"Today reminded me of something I heard a wise man say recently," said Pete. "The highest purpose is about building a life and sharing it with others."[3]

"Another quote from Rick?" asked Melissa.

"Not quite. I was watching an online class last night with Arthur C. Brooks and his guest lecturer, the Dalai Lama."

Melissa was quiet for a moment. "You know, I think I might be becoming envious of your life. I feel like I'm getting burned out. Maybe it's time for me to think about a second act, too. But I don't know where I would even start."

"Well, I know a guy...," said Pete.

AFTERWORD

GO WIN YOUR RETIREMENT GAME

What's the path from here that's right for you? The new life Pete created is unlikely to be your path. But the principles he learned are valuable in crafting your own. It's time to focus on *your* Retirement Game. You're well aware of the nine opponents you may encounter, and you're armed with game plans for each.

You know how to outfox Boredom, evade the Status Quo, and circumvent Inertia. You're prepared to conquer Uncertainty, vanquish Loneliness, and break free from other people's Expectations, when they're unhelpful. And you're ready to sidestep Overwhelm, outmaneuver unrealistic Obligations, and reject Drifting without direction.

Let's review how you can be proactive in creating your new life. Note which of these nine opportunities resonate most with you:

1. Awaken your Curiosity by keenly observing the world around you.
   A. Be inquisitive about what interests you. Investigate how different things work.
   B. Make a list of things that intrigue you but that you haven't had time, until now, to look into or to study. Highlight the first one you're excited to dive into.
   C. Remember to be curious about *You*. You may know yourself well, but remember, you've never been at this stage of life before, and you're still evolving. Observe how you respond to this transition, how you're adapting, and how you're continuing your personal growth.
2. Befriend Change by giving yourself time to adjust to the transition you'll be making.
   A. Embrace the most important project on your list: the New You.
   B. Craft a list of what it's time to let go of as you enter this new phase.
   C. Make a separate list of new things you want to take up or just take for a test drive.
3. Foster Connectivity by deepening your most important relationships and seizing opportunities to build new ones.
   A. Find your new tribe.
   B. Look for new activities that will help you meet new people.
   C. Remember to value your "weak ties," as they can be helpful relationships in their own way and become a gateway to others.
4. Ignite Creativity by stepping outside your comfort zone.
   A. Create a basic structure and habits for a new life, but leave space for play, exploring, and experimenting.

B. Try different activities that nudge you to learn something totally new.

C. Seek various ways to engage with the arts, including appreciating and creating.

D. Challenge yourself to think of novel ways to solve problems in daily life by leveraging your experience and wisdom.

5. Develop Acceptance of the realities of your new life after full-time work.

   A. What are the things you'll miss about work?

   B. How can you replace them and find new ways to get the same benefits?

   C. What are the hardest challenges you'll face that are beyond your control? How will you address them?

6. Create Clarity about your new direction by assembling four building blocks of activities and interests. You're graduating to a new phase of life. Write down *one thing* you want to do or try out in these foundational areas of your new life:

   A. Fitness

   B. Learning

   C. A new version of Work or Service

   D. Fun

Next to each one, jot down your next step with a deadline you're committed to hit.

7. Pursue Challenge in your new life. When you stop learning, you stop growing.

   A. Do the things you're planning to do in retirement appear to have the right degree of challenge, so you're engaged and growing? Are they challenging without becoming overwhelming or overly stressful?

B. Identify one area of life or a pursuit where you'd like to stretch yourself a bit.

C. What's an activity you love that you'd like to take up a notch?

D. What's a new pursuit that will push you just the right amount?

8. Detect a Calling, if there's one for you.

A. Have there been calls for a second act or an interest you've not pursued? Is now the time?

B. Use the gift of time that your new life offers to regularly allow for quiet. Don't get so busy with new activities that you can't hear the right one calling to you.

9. Discover new Purposes by experimenting with meaningful activities.

A. What's most important now?

B. How can your talents, skills, experience, and wisdom be redirected and make a difference for others?

You may be retiring, but you're not done yet—*It's your time.* Create the new life you've earned with imagination, experimentation, and a sense of adventure.

ACKNOWLEDGEMENTS

Thank you to my wife Pat, for putting up with me for forty-one years and counting, and for our children, Sarah, Joanna, Rebecca, and Matt, who each encouraged me during this project in different ways.

To my coaching clients, whose courage to chart their own course inspires me.

To Tom Lane, whose editorial expertise and recommendations made all the difference.

To Debbie Weill and Donald Miller, whose coaching and teaching helped launch this book.

To the many educators who've helped me learn and grow as an executive coach over the past thirteen years: my executive coach Ruth Orenstein; the faculty of the Columbia University Coaching Certification Program and the Middlesex University Master's program; David Peterson and David Goldsmith at 7

Paths Forward; my fellow coaches in the ACE and Virtuoso programs; Bill Burnett and Dave Evans, whose Designing Your Life approach helps my clients envision and bring their next chapters to life; BJ Fogg, PhD, Director of the Behavior Design Lab at Stanford, whose breakthrough Tiny Habits Method has helped me personally and professionally; and Tim Gallwey, whose Inner Game books I often recommend to clients.

To the coaches who took time to meet and share their wisdom with me for a master's thesis on coaching, especially Marshall Goldsmith, Brian Underhill, Jenny Rogers, Peter Haddon, Scott Eblin, and Karol Wasylyshyn, who shared a unique coaching technique that Pete's three paintings from his art class honors.

Thank you to Denis Wuestman and Bev Bachel for their contributions to Retirement Wisdom and to the guests I've interviewed on the *Retirement Wisdom* podcast. Special thanks to those guests who joined us when it was just beginning in 2017 and helped launch the podcast, including Fritz Gilbert, Thelma Reese, Melissa Davey, David Ekerdt, Emily Esfahani Smith, Nicole Maestas, Nell Painter, Dorie Clark, Alan Castel, Catherine Collinson, Kerry Hannon, and Charlotte Japp.

I've had opportunities to learn about successful aging and the power of intergenerational collaboration in recent years from a diverse group of talented people. Thank you to Leah Buturain and her meaningful class Mindful Aging at USC; Cindy Cox-Roman, my classmate at USC; the members of the Life Planning Network in Philadelphia; The Encore Network Multigenerational Roundtable; and Charley Timmins and his Friday morning virtual learning group in Philadelphia.

And thank you to the people I interviewed for this book whose input provided valuable background. While this book contains client stories, they are based on a composite of multiple client experiences and do not represent a specific individual.

RESOURCES

RECOMMENDED READING

People often ask me what books they should read on retirement. Here are recommendations to choose from. I've learned that some of the best books for retirement aren't specifically about retirement, but their key points are relevant and useful.

RETIREMENT

Blanchard, K., & Shaevitz, M. (2015). *Refire! Don't Retire: Make the Rest of Your Life the Best of Your Life.* Berrett-Koehler Publishers

Bratter, B., & Dennis, H. (2008). *Project Renewment: The First Retirement Model for Career Women.* Simon and Schuster.

Edleson, H. (2021). 12 *Ways to Retire on Less: Planning an Affordable Future.* Rowman & Littlefield.

Gilbert, F. (2020). *The Keys to a Successful Retirement*. Rockridge Press.

Kaufman, T., & Hiland, B. (2021). *Retiring? Your Next Chapter Is about Much More Than Money*. Houndstooth Press.

O'Neill, B. (2020). *Flipping a Switch: Your Guide to Happiness and Financial Security In Later Life*. Atlantic Publishing Company.

Silver, M. P. (2018). *Retirement and Its Discontents*. Columbia University Press.

CRAFTING A NEW LIFE

Burnett, W., Burnett, B., & Evans, D. J. (2016). *Designing Your Life: How to Build a Well-lived, Joyful Life*. Knopf.

Clinton, M. (2021). *ROAR: Into the Second Half of Your life (before It's Too Late)*. Atria Books/Beyond Words.

Damon, W. (2021). *A Round of Golf with My Father: The New Psychology of Exploring Your Past to Make Peace with Your Present*. Templeton Press.

Johnson, B.D. (2021). *The Future You: How to Create the Life You Always Wanted*. Harper One.

Kraemer, H. (2020). *Your 168: Finding Purpose and satisfaction in a values-based life*. Wiley.

Lordan, G. (2021). *Think Big: Take Small Steps and Build the Future You Want.*

Robin, A. (2021). *Tapas Life: A Rich and Rewarding Life after Your Long Career.* (n.d.).

Weinstein, l. (2017). *Write, Open, Act: An Intentional Life Planning Workbook.* Intentional Life Planning, LLC.

Weiss, A., & Goldsmith, M. (2017). *Lifestorming: Creating Meaning and Achievement in Your Career and Life.* Wiley.

LIVING WELL

Boardman, S. (2021). *Everyday Vitality: Turning Stress into Strength.* Penguin Random House.

Brooks, A. C. (2022). *From Strength to Strength: Finding Success, Happiness, and Deep Purpose In the Second Half of Life.* Portfolio/Penguin.

Goldsmith, M. (2022). *The Earned Life: Lose Regret, Choose Fulfillment.* Currency.

Kabat-Zinn, J. (2006). *Mindfulness for Beginners.* Louisville, CO: Sounds True.

Sanderson, C. (2019). *The Positive Shift: Mastering Mindset to Improve Happiness, Health, and Longevity.* Ben Bella Books.

AGING WELL

Gratton, L., & Scott, A. J. (2016). *The 100-Year Life: Living and Working in An Age Of Longevity*. Bloomsbury Publishing.

Castel, A. D. (2018). *Better with Age: The Psychology of Successful Aging*. Oxford University Press.

Chittister, J. (2008). *The Gift of Years: Growing Old Gracefully*. Darton, Longman and Todd.

Rohr, R. (2011). *Falling Upward: A Spirituality for the Two Halves of Life*. Jossey-Bass.

Spiers, P. (2012). *Master Class: Living Longer, Stronger, and Happier*. Center Street.

CREATIVITY, JOY, AND FUN

Cameron, J., & Lively, E. (2016). *It's Never Too Late to Begin Again: Discovering Creativity and Meaning at Midlife and Beyond*. TarcherPerigee.

Lee, I. F. (2018). *Joyful: The Surprising Power of Ordinary Things to Create Extraordinary Happiness*. Random House.

Price, C. (2022). *The Power Of Fun: Why Fun Is the Key to a Happy and Healthy Life*. Random House.

CHANGE

Fogg, B. J. (2019). *Tiny Habits: The Small Changes that Change Everything*. Eamon Dolan Books.

Gallwey, W. T. (1975). *The Inner Game of Tennis: The Ultimate Guide to the Mental Side of Peak Performance*. Pan Books.

PURPOSE AND MEANING

Smith, E. E. (2017). *The Power of Meaning: Crafting a Life That Matters*. Random House.

Stretcher, V. (2016). *Life on Purpose: How Living for What Matters Most Changes Everything*. HarperOne.

Reese, T., & Kittredge, B. J. (2020). *How Seniors Are Saving The World: Retirement Activism to the Rescue!* Rowman & Littlefield Publishers.

ONLINE RESOURCES
THE RETIREMENT MANIFESTO

A wealth of valuable information: theretirementmanifesto.com

RENEWMENT

A forum and community of career women ages fifty-five-plus that supports their transition from work to retirement with over forty groups worldwide: renewment.org

TINY HABITS

BJ Fogg's free five-day email course: tinyhabits.com

THE RETIREMENT WISDOM PODCAST

A free Retirement School with weekly interviews by the author to help you plan for the non-financial side of retirement. Browse all the episodes at retirementwisdom.com/the-retirement-wisdom-podcast/ and follow the podcast on Apple Podcasts or wherever you listen to podcasts.

ABOUT THE AUTHOR

JOE CASEY is an executive coach who also helps people design their new lives after they retire at Retirement Wisdom.® Before becoming a coach in 2009, Joe spent twenty-six years at Merrill Lynch, where he was Senior Vice President, Head of HR for Global Markets and Investment Banking, and was previously Managing Director and the Chief Operating Officer of Global HR. Joe earned master's degrees from the University of Pennsylvania and Middlesex University in the UK, a BA from the University of Massachusetts at Amherst, and his coaching certification from Columbia University. In 2018, he earned a third master's degree, this time in gerontology from the University of Southern California, to advance his understanding of the life course and to inform his retirement coaching.

Joe has been quoted in publications including *The Wall Street Journal, Business Insider, MarketWatch, US News & World Report, Kiplinger, The Atlantic, The New York Times,* and *CNBC.com* on topics including retirement and encore careers. Joe has run thirteen marathons in cities including Philadelphia, San

Francisco, and Boston. In college, Joe was a cartoonist for his college newspaper and believes a well-developed sense of humor is one of the most valuable assets to bring to retirement.

Today, in addition to his work with clients, Joe hosts *The Retirement Wisdom* Podcast, ranked in the top 1.5 percent globally in popularity by Listen Notes. He also knows a great retirement takes smart planning. An experienced coach can help you create the life you want after your primary career. Learn more at retirementwisdom.com

NOTES

INTRODUCTION

1   Employee Benefit Research Institute and Greenwald Associates. (2021, April). "2021 Retirement Confidence Survey." Ebri.org. https://www.ebri.org/docs/default-source/rcs/2021-rcs/2021-rcs-summary-report.pdf?sfvrsn=bd83a2f_2.

CHAPTER ONE

1   "The Holmes-Rahe Stress Inventory." (2020, April 22). The American Institute of Stress. Stress.org. https://www.stress.org/holmes-rahe-stress-inventory.

2   O'Neill, B. (2020). Flipping a Switch: Your Guide to Happiness and Financial Security in Later Life. Atlantic Publishing Company.

3   Baumeister, R. F., Bratslavsky, E., Finkenauer, C., & Vohs, K. D. (2001). Bad Is Stronger Than Good. *Review of General Psychology, 5*(4), 323–370.

4   Fogg, B. J. (2019). *Tiny Habits: The Small Changes That Change Everything*. Houghton Mifflin Harcourt.

5   Blanchard, K., & Shaevitz, M. (2015). *Refire! Don't Retire: Make the Rest of Your Life the Best of Your Life*. Berrett-Koehler Publishers.

6   Stephan, Y. (2009). Openness to Experience and Active Older Adults' Life Satisfaction: A Trait and Facet-Level Analysis. *Personality and Individual Differences, 47*(6), 637–641.

7   Jackson, J. J., Hill, P. L., Payne, B. R., Roberts, B. W., & Stine-Morrow, E. A. (2012). Can An Old Dog Learn (and Want to Experience) New Tricks? Cognitive Training Increases Openness to Experience in Older Adults. *Psychology and Aging, 27*(2), 286.

CHAPTER TWO

1   Elpidio, A. (2018). The Good of Boredom. *Philosophical Psychology, 31*(3), 323–351.

2   Westgate, E. (2019). Are We Bored Yet? A Lifespan Perspective on the MAC Model of Boredom and Cognitive Engagement. https://psyarxiv.com/4h6et/.

3   Renner, B. (2019, March 19). *Retirement Blues: Average Retiree Grows Bored After Just One Year, Survey Finds.* https://www.studyfinds.org/most-people-grow-bored-retirement-just-one-year/.

4   Ducharme, J. (2019, January 4). Being Bored Can Be Good for You—If You Do It Right. Here's How. *Time.* https://time.com/5480002/benefits-of-boredom/.

5   Moynihan, A. B., Igou, E. R., & van Tilburg, W. A. (2017). Boredom Increases Impulsiveness. *Social Psychology, 48*(5), 293–309.

6   Westgate, Erin C. (2020, March 27). Six Things You Can Do to Cope with Boredom at a Time of Social Distancing. *The Conversation.* https://theconversation.com/6-things-you-can-do-to-cope-with-boredom-at-a-time-of-social-distancing-134734.

7   Mann, S. (2017). *The Science of Boredom: The Upside (and Downside) of Downtime.* Robinson.

8   Mann, S. (2017).

9   Kashdan, T. (2009). *Curious? Discover the Missing Ingredient to a Fulfilling Life* (p. 159). William Morrow & Co.

10   Kashdan, T. B., & Silvia, P. J. (2009). Curiosity and Interest: The Benefits of Thriving on Novelty and Challenge. *Oxford Handbook of Positive Psychology, 2,* p. 368.

11   Brink, A. (2008). *Curiosity, Personal Growth Initiative, and Life Satisfaction in Older Adults.* The Chicago School of Professional Psychology.

12   Covey, S. R. (1989). *The 7 Habits of Highly Effective People.* Simon and Schuster.

13   Kashdan & Silvia (2009).

14   Gratton, L., & Scott, A. J. (2016). *The 100-Year Life: Living and Working in an Age of Longevity.* Bloomsbury Publishing.

15   de Gobbi Porto, F. H., Fox, A. M., Tusch, E. S., Sorond, F., Mohammed, A. H., & Daffner, K. R. (2015). In Vivo Evidence for Neuroplasticity in Older Adults. *Brain Research Bulletin, 114,* 56–61.

16 Dweck, C. S. (2008). *Mindset: The New Psychology of Success*. Random House Digital, Inc.

17 Popova, M. (2014, January 24). Fixed Versus Growth: The Two Basic Mindsets that Shape Our Lives. *Brain Pickings*. https://www.brainpickings.org/2014/01/29/carol-dweck-mindset/.

18 Gallwey, W. T. (1975). *The Inner Game of Tennis: The Ultimate Guide to the Mental Side of Peak Performance*. Pan Books.

CHAPTER THREE

1 The Secret to Life is Just Three Words, According to Alan Alda. (2020, June 1). Considerable.com. https://www.considerable.com/health/aging/mash-star-alan-alda-advice-younger-self/.

2 Wang, M., Henkens, K., & van Solinge, H. (2011). Retirement Adjustment: A Review of Theoretical and Empirical Advancements. *American Psychologist, 66*(3), 204.

3 Van Solinge, H., & Henkens, K. (2008). Adjustment to and Satisfaction with Retirement: Two of a Kind? *Psychology and Aging, 23*(2), 429.

4 Calvo, E., Haverstick, K., & Sass, S. A. (2009). Gradual Retirement, Sense of Control, and Retirees' Happiness. *Research on Aging, 31*(1), 112–135.

5 Prochaska, J. O., & DiClemente, C. C. (1982). Transtheoretical Therapy: Toward a More Integrative Model of Change. *Psychotherapy: Theory, Research & Practice, 19*(3), 276.

6 Levitin, D. J. (2020). *Successful Aging: A Neuroscientist Explores the Power and Potential of Our Lives*. Penguin.

7 Bleidorn, W., & Schwaba, T. (2018). Retirement is associated with change in self-esteem. *Psychology and Aging, 33*(4), 586.

8 Froidevaux, A., Hirschi, A., & Wang, M. (2016). The Role of Mattering as an Overlooked Key Challenge in Retirement Planning and Adjustment. *Journal of Vocational Behavior, 94*, 57–69.

9 Lewis, M. (2016). *The Undoing Project: A Friendship that Changed the World*. Penguin UK.

10 Kahneman, D., Knetsch, J. L., & Thaler, R. H. (1991). Anomalies: The Endowment Effect, Loss Aversion, and Status Quo Bias. *Journal of Economic Perspectives, 5*(1), 193–206.

11 Xiao, Q., LAM, C. S. E., Piara, M., & Feldman, G. (2020). Revisiting Status Quo Bias: Replication of Samuelson and Zeckhauser (1988). *Meta-Psychology, 5*. https://open.lnu.se/index.php/metapsychology/article/view/2470/2535.

12 Samuelson, W., & Zeckhauser, R. (1988). Status Quo Bias in Decision Making. *Journal of Risk and Uncertainty, 1*(1), 759.

13 Baltes, P. B. (1987). Theoretical Propositions of Life-Span Developmental Psychology: On the Dynamics Between Growth and Decline. *Developmental Psychology, 23*(5), 611.

14 Baltes, M. M., & Carstensen, L. L. (1996). The Process of Successful Ageing. *Ageing & Society, 16*(4), 397–422.

15 Baltes & Carstensen, p. 405.

16 Bye, D., & Pushkar, D. (2009). How Need for Cognition and Perceived Control Are Differentially Linked to Emotional Outcomes in the Transition to Retirement. *Motivation and Emotion, 33*(3), 322.

17 Infurna, F. J., Gerstorf, D., Ram, N., Schupp, J., Wagner, G. G., & Heckhausen, J. (2016). Maintaining Perceived Control with Unemployment Facilitates Future Adjustment. *Journal of Vocational Behavior, 93*, 103–119.

18 Wood, W., & Neal, D. T. (2007). A New Look at Habits and the Habit-Goal Interface. *Psychological Review, 114*(4), 843.

19 Brooks, A. C. (2020, April 9). The Three Equations for a Happy Life, Even During a Pandemic. *The Atlantic.* https://www.theatlantic.com/family/archive/2020/04/how-increase-happiness-according-research/609619/

20 Fogg, BJ. (2019). *Tiny Habits: The Small Changes that Change Everything.* Houghton Mifflin Harcourt.

CHAPTER FOUR

1 Gawande, A. (2009). Hellhole. *The New Yorker, 85,* 7–30.

2 Townsend, K. C., & McWhirter, B. T. (2005). Connectedness: A Review of the Literature with Implications for Counseling, Assessment, and Research. *Journal of Counseling & Development, 83*(2), 191–201.

3 O'Rourke, H. M., Collins, L., & Sidani, S. (2018). Interventions to Address Social Connectedness and Loneliness for Older Adults: A Scoping Review. *BMC Geriatrics, 18*(1), 214.

4 Cruwys, T., Haslam, C., Steffens, N. K., Haslam, S. A., Fong, P., & Lam, B. C. (2019). Friendships that Money Can Buy: Financial Security Protects Health in Retirement by Enabling Social Connectedness. *BMC Geriatrics, 19*(1), 319.

5 Ianzito, C. (2020, June 16). Former Surgeon General Vivek Murthy on the Loneliness Epidemic. *AARP.* https://www.aarp.org/health/healthy-living/info-2020/vivek-murthy-loneliness.html.

6 Cacioppo, J. T., & Cacioppo, S. (2018). The Growing Problem of Loneliness. *The Lancet, 391*(10119), 426.

7   Soni, V. (2019). The Loneliness Crisis on US College Campuses. *The Los Angeles Times*, A18.

8   Cacioppo & Cacioppo (2018).

9   PM Launches Government's First Loneliness Strategy. (2018, Oct.). Gov.UK. https://www.gov.uk/ government/news/pm-launches-governments-first-loneliness-strategy

10 Murthy, V. (2017, Sept.). Connecting at Work. We're More Connected than Ever, but Loneliness is Epidemic. *Harvard Business Review*.

11 Murthy (2017).

12 Livingston, G. (2019, July 3). *On Average, Older Adults Spend Half of Their Waking Hours Alone*. Pew Research Center. https://www.pewresearch.org/fact-tank/2019/07/03/ on-average-older-adults-spend-over-half-their-waking-hours-alone/.

13 Huxhold, O., Fiori, K. L., Webster, N. J., & Antonucci, T. C. (2020). The Strength of Weaker Ties: An Underexplored Resource for Maintaining Emotional Well-Being in Later Life. *The Journals of Gerontology: Series B*.

14 Smith, S. (2010). *Social Connectedness and Retirement* (No. 10/255). Department of Economics, University of Bristol, UK.

15 Schwaba, T., & Bleidorn, W. (2019). Personality Trait Development Across the Transition to Retirement. *Journal of Personality and Social Psychology, 116*(4), 651.

16 Barreto, M., Victor, C., Hammond, C., Eccles, A., Richins, M. T., & Qualter, P. (2020). Loneliness Around the World: Age, Gender, and Cultural Differences in Loneliness. *Personality and Individual Differences*, 110066.

17 Shin, O., Park, S., Amano, T., Kwon, E., & Kim, B. (2020, Dec.). Nature of Retirement and Loneliness: The Moderating Roles of Social Support. *Journal of Applied Gerontology, 39*(12), 1292–1302.

18 Smith (2010).

19 Comi, S. L., Cottini, E., & Lucifora, C. (2020). *The Effect of Retirement on Social Relationships: New Evidence from SHARE* (No. def088). Università Cattolica del Sacro Cuore, Dipartimenti e Istituti di Scienze Economiche (DISCE).

20 Comi et al. (2020).

21 Carstensen, L. L. (1992). Social and Emotional Patterns in Adulthood: Support for Socioemotional Selectivity Theory. *Psychology and Aging, 7*(3), 331–338.

22 Crowley, J. E. (2019). Gray Divorce: Explaining Midlife Marital Splits. *Journal of Women & Aging, 31*(1), 49–72.

23 Leslie, I. (2020, July 2). Why Your 'Weak-Tie' Friendships May Mean More than You Think. *BBC.com*. https://www.bbc.com/worklife/article/20200701-why-your-weak-tie-friendships-may-mean-more-than-you-think.

24 Volpe, A. (2020, May 6). Why You Need a Network of Low Stakes, Casual Friendships. Weak Ties Can Offer Strong Rewards. *The New York Times*. https://www.nytimes.com/2019/05/06/smarter-living/why-you-need-a-network-of-low-stakes-casual-friendships.html.

25 Feiler, B. (2017, October 12). Should Your Spouse Be Your Best Friend? *The New York Times*. https://www.nytimes.com/2017/10/12/style/should-your-spouse-be-your-best-friend.html.

26 Grover, S., & Helliwell, J. F. (2019). How's Life at Home? New Evidence on Marriage and the Set Point for Happiness. *Journal of Happiness Studies, 20*(2), 373–390.

CHAPTER FIVE

1 Cameron, J., & Lively, E. (2016). *It's Never Too Late to Begin Again: Discovering Creativity and Meaning at Midlife and Beyond*. Artist's Way.

2 Sternberg, R. J., & Lubart, T. I. (1999). The Concept of Creativity: Prospects and Paradigms. *Handbook of Creativity*, 1, 3–15.

3 Fraser K. D., O'Rourke H.M., Wiens H., Lai J., Howell C. and Brett-MacLean, P. (2015). A Scoping Review of Research on the Arts, Aging, and Quality of Life. *The Gerontologist 55*, 719–729.

4 Cohen, G.D. (2006). Research on Creativity and Aging: The Positive Impact of the Arts on Health and Illness. Generations, 30(1), 7–15.

5 Cohen, G. (2000). *The Creative Age: Awakening Human Potential in the Second Half of Life.* (pp. 92–93). New York: Harper-Collins.

6 Tymoszuk, U., Perkins, R., Spiro, N., Williamon, A., & Fancourt, D. (2019). Longitudinal Associations Between Short-Term, Repeated, and Sustained Arts Engagement and Well-Being Outcomes in Older Adults. *The Journals of Gerontology: Series B.*

7 Adams-Price, C. E., Nadorff, D. K., Morse, L. W., Davis, K. T., & Stearns, M. A. (2018). The Creative Benefits Scale: Connecting Generativity to Life Satisfaction. *The International Journal of Aging and Human Development, 86*(3), 242–265.

8 Cameron & Lively (2016).

9 Oxford English Dictionary. Lexico.com. https://www.lexico.com/en/definition/inertia.

10 Mann, S., & Cadman, R. (2014). Does Being Bored Make Us More Creative? *Creativity Research Journal, 26*(2), 165–173.

11   Castel, A. D. (2018). *Better with Age: The Psychology of Successful Aging* (pp. 70–71). Oxford University Press.

12   Weber, B. (2009, November 12). Gene D. Cohen, Geriatric Psychiatrist, Dies at 65. *The New York Times.* https://www.nytimes.com/2009/11/12/us/12cohen.html.

13   Fehr, R. (2013). Retirement and Creativity in Wang, M. (Ed.). (2013). *The Oxford Handbook of Retirement* (pp. 588–602). Oxford University Press.

14   Fehr, R. (2012, Jan.). Is Retirement Always Stressful? The Potential Impact of Creativity. *The American Psychologist, 67*(1), 76–77.

15   Schwartz, T. (2011, Nov. 14). How to Think Creatively. *Harvard Business Review.*

CHAPTER SIX

1   Burns, D. D. (1999). *The Feeling Good Handbook* (p. 768). New York: Plume.

2   Lucas, L. (2021, January 14). Why Do People Spend the Way They Do in Retirement? Findings from EBRI's spending in retirement survey. Employee Benefit Research Institute. https://www.ebri.org/content/why-do-people-spend-the-way-they-do-in-retirement-findings-from-ebri-s-spending-in-retirement-survey.

3   Feiler, B. (2020). *Life Is in the Transitions: Mastering Change at Any Age.* Penguin Press.

4   Ng, R., Allore, H. G., Monin, J. K., & Levy, B. R. (2016). Retirement As Meaningful: Positive Retirement Stereotypes Associated with Longevity. *Journal of Social Issues, 72*(1), 69–85.

5   Ng et al. (2020), p. 69.

6   Figueira, D. A. M., Haddad, M. D. C. L., Gvozd, R., & Pissinati, P. D. S. C. (2017). Retirement Decision-Making Influenced by Family and Work Relationships. *Revista Brasileira de Geriatria e Gerontologia, 20*(2), 206–213.

7   Paskov, M., Gërxhani, K., & van de Werfhorst, H. G. (2017). Giving up on the Joneses? The Relationship Between Income Inequality and Status-Seeking. *European Sociological Review, 33*(1), 112–123.

8   Carson, S. H., & Langer, E. J. (2006). Mindfulness and Self-Acceptance. *Journal of Rational-Emotive and Cognitive-Behavior Therapy, 24*(1), 29–43.

9   Peck, M. D., & Merighi, J. R. (2007). The Relation of Social Comparison to Subjective Well-Being and Health Status in Older Adults. *Journal of Human Behavior in the Social Environment, 16*(3), 121–142.

10   Ellis, A., & Harper, R. A. (1961). *A Guide to Rational Living.* Prentice-Hall.

11 Tobias, K. (2013, October 25). *Milestone Misery? Stop Shoulding on Yourself.* The Albert Ellis Institute. https://albertellis.org/milestone-misery-stop-shoulding/.

12 Friedman, S. D. (2008). *Total Leadership: Be a Better Leader, Have a Richer Life.* Harvard Business Press.

13 Langer, E. J. (2014). *Mindfulness.* Da Capo Lifelong Books.

14 Carson, S. H., & Langer, E. J. (2006). Mindfulness and Self-Acceptance. *Journal of Rational-Emotive and Cognitive-Behavior Therapy, 24*(1), 2943.

15 Carson S. & Langer, E. (2006). pp. 39–41.

16 Ng, R., Allore, H. G., & Levy, B. R. (2020). Self-Acceptance and Interdependence Promote Longevity: Evidence from a 20-Year Prospective Cohort Study. *International Journal of Environmental Research and Public Health, 17*(16), 5980.

17 Blanton, K. (2018, November 15.) *Why Couples Retire Together—or Don't.* Center for Retirement Research at Boston College. https://squaredawayblog.bc.edu/squared-away/why-couples-retire-together-or-dont/.

CHAPTER SEVEN

1 Bandura, A. (2006). Toward a Psychology of Human Agency. *Perspectives on Psychological Science, 1*(2), 164-180.

2 American Psychological Association. (2020, August 20). The Great Unknown: 10 Tips for Dealing with the Stress of Uncertainty. https://www.apa.org/topics/stress-uncertainty.

3 Aschwanden, C. (2020, September 12). Uncertainty Fuels Anxiety, Causing Your Mind to Conjure up Scary Scenarios. *Washington Post.* https://www.washingtonpost.com/health/covid-anxiety-how-to-cope-uncertainty/2020/09/11/fae65832-d1b2-11ea-8d32-1ebf4e9d8eod_story.html

4 Dictionary, M. W. (2002). Merriam-Webster. https://www.merriam-webster.com/dictionary/uncertainty.

5 American Psychological Association. (2020, August 20). The Great Unknown: 10 Tips for Dealing with the Stress of Uncertainty. https://www.apa.org/topics/stress-uncertainty.

6 Moffatt, S., & Heaven, B. (2017). 'Planning for Uncertainty': Narratives on Retirement Transition Experiences. *Ageing & Society, 37*(5), 879-898.

7 Grupe, D. W., & Nitschke, J. B. (2013). Uncertainty and Anticipation in Anxiety: An Integrated Neurobiological and Psychological Perspective. *Nature Reviews Neuroscience, 14*(7), 488-501.

8 Moffatt, S., & Heaven, B. (2017). 'Planning for Uncertainty': Narratives on Retirement Transition Experiences. *Ageing & Society, 37*(5), 879-898.

9 Johnson, B.D. (2021, June 9). The Future You—Brian David Johnson. *The Retirement Wisdom Podcast.* https://www.retirementwisdom.com/podcasts/the-future-you-brian-david-johnson/.

10 Haggbloom, S. J., Warnick, R., Warnick, J. E., Jones, V. K., Yarbrough, G. L., Russell, T. M., & Monte, E. (2002). The 100 Most Eminent Psychologists of the 20th Century. *Review of General Psychology, 6*(2), 139–152.

11 Bandura, A. (1977). Self-Efficacy: Toward a Unifying Theory of Behavior Change. *Psychological Review,* 191–215.

12 Bandura, A. (1994). Self-Efficacy. In V. S. Ramachaudran (Ed.), *Encyclopedia of Human Behavior* (Vol. 4, pp. 71–81). New York: Academic Press. (Reprinted in H. Friedman [Ed.], *Encyclopedia of Mental Health.* San Diego: Academic Press, 1998).

13 Hyde, M., Cheshire-Allen, M., Damman, M., Henkens, K., Platts, L., Pritchard, K., & Reed, C. (2018). The Experience of the Transition to Retirement: Rapid Evidence Review. http://orca.cf.ac.uk/118616/7/transition-to-retirement.pdf.

14 Hitlin, S., & Elder Jr, G. H. (2006). Agency: An Empirical Model of an Abstract Concept. *Advances in Life Course Research, 11,* 33–67.

15 Topa, G., & Pra, I. (2018). Retirement Adjustment Quality: Optimism and Self-Efficacy as Antecedents of Resource Accumulation. *Applied Research in Quality of Life, 13*(4), 1015–1035.

16 Damman, M., Henkens, K., & Kalmijn, M. (2015). Missing Work After Retirement: The Role of Life Histories in the Retirement Adjustment Process. *The Gerontologist, 55*(5), 802–813.

17 Wang, M., & Hesketh, B. (2012). Achieving Well-Being in Retirement: Recommendations from 20 Years of Research. *SIOP White Paper Series, 1*(1), 11–22.

18 Damman et al. (2015). p. 811.

19 Bandura, A. (2006).

CHAPTER EIGHT

1 Godin, S. (2020, October 8). *The Cold Open. Seth's Blog.com.* Retrieved from https://setho.blog/2020/10/the-cold-open/

2 Cowen, T. (2017). *The Complacent Class: The Self-Defeating Quest for the American Dream.* St. Martin's Press.

3 Cowen, p. 2.

4 Cowen, p. 12.

5   1440 Multiversity. (2019, May 11). Life Begins at the End of Your Comfort Zone: Talking with Neale Donald Walsch. https://www.1440.org/blog/life-begins-at-the-end-of-your-comfort-zone-talking-with-neale-donald-walsch.

6   Complacency. (n.d.). *Merriam Webster.* Retrieved from https://www.merriam-webster.com/dictionary/complacency.

7   Stebbins, R. A. (2013). *Planning Your Time in Retirement: How to Cultivate a Leisure Lifestyle to Suit Your Needs and Interests.* Lanham, MD: Rowman & Littlefield.

8   Seriousleisure.net (n.d). Retrieved from https://www.seriousleisure.net/concepts.html.

9   Stebbins (2013).

10 Complacency. (n.d.). *Merriam Webster.* Retrieved from https://www.merriam-webster.com/dictionary/complacency.

11 Stebbins, R. A. (2017). *Leisure's Legacy: Challenging the Commonsense View of Free Time.* Springer.

12 Bunea, E. (2020, July 3). "Grace Under Pressure": How CEOs Use Serious Leisure to Cope with the Demands of their Job. *Frontiers in Psychology, 11.*

13 Bunea, E. (2019, May). *Why Leaders Should Take Their Leisure Seriously.* TED Conferences. https://www.ted.com/talks/emilia_bunea_why_leaders_should_take_their_leisure_seriously_jan_2019?language=en.

14 Bunea (2020).

15 Bunea (2020).

16 Talmage, C. A., Hansen, R. J., Knopf, R. C., Thaxton, S. P., McTague, R., & Moore, D. B. (2019). Unleashing the Value of Lifelong Learning Institutes: Research and Practice Insights from a National Survey of Osher Lifelong Learning Institutes. *Adult Education Quarterly, 69*(3), 184–206.

17 Kim, J. E., & Moen, P. (2002). Retirement Transitions, Gender, and Psychological Well-Being: A Life-Course, Ecological Model. *The Journals of Gerontology Series B: Psychological Sciences and Social Sciences, 57*(3), 212–222.

18 Donaldson, T., Earl, J. K., & Muratore, A. M. (2010). Extending the Integrated Model of Retirement Adjustment: Incorporating Mastery and Retirement Planning. *Journal of Vocational Behavior, 77*(2), 279–289.

CHAPTER NINE

1   Palmer, P. J. (1999). *Let Your Life Speak: Listening for the Voice of Vocation.* John Wiley & Sons.

2   Wrzesniewski, A., McCauley, C. R., Rozin, P., & Schwartz, B. (1997). Jobs, Careers, and Callings: People's Relations to Their Work. *Journal of Research in Personality*, 31, 21–33.

3   Hall, D. T., & Chandler, D. E. (2005). Psychological Success: When the Career is a Calling. *Journal of Organizational Behavior: The International Journal of Industrial, Occupational and Organizational Psychology and Behavior*, 26(2), 155–176.

4   Wrzesniewski, A. Callings. In Yaden, D. B., McCall, T. D., & Ellens, J. H. (Eds.). (2015). *Being Called: Scientific, Secular, and Sacred Perspectives: Scientific, Secular, and Sacred Perspectives* (p. 32). ABC-CLIO.

5   Schuster, J. (2003). *Answering Your Call: A Guide for Living Your Deepest Purpose* (p. 13). Berrett-Koehler Publishers.

6   Duffy, R. D., & Dik, B. J. (2013). Research on Calling: What Have We Learned and Where Are We Going? *Journal of Vocational Behavior*, 83(3), 429.

7   Duffy, R. D., Torrey, C. L., England, J., & Tebbe, E. A. (2017). Calling in Retirement: A Mixed Methods Study. *The Journal of Positive Psychology*, 12(4), 399–413; Duffy, R. D., Bott, E. M., Allan, B. A., Torrey, C. L., & Dik, B. J. (2012). Perceiving a Calling, Living a Calling, and Job Satisfaction: Testing a Moderated, Multiple Mediator Model. *Journal of Counseling Psychology*, 59(1), 50.

8   Vough, H. C., Bataille, C. D., Sargent, L., & Lee, M. D. (2016). Next-Gen Retirement. *Harvard Business Review*, 94(6), 19.

9   Duffy et al. (2017), p. 404.

10 Ware, B. (2012). *The Top Five Regrets of the Dying: A Life Transformed by the Dearly Departing*. Hay House, Inc.

11 Dyer, W. W. (2016). *10 Secrets for Success and Inner Peace*. Hay House, Inc.

12 Schuster, J. (2003), p. 17.

13 Krznaric, R. (2020, October 28). Three Ideas for a Fuller Life. BBC.com https://www.bbc.com/culture/article/20201027-how-to-live-your-best-life.

14 Isay, D., & Millett, M. (2017). *Callings: The Purpose and Passion of Work*. Penguin.

15 Schuster (2003), pp. 40–41.

16 Barnes, H., & Parry, J. (2004). Renegotiating Identity and Relationships: Men and Women's Adjustments to Retirement. *Ageing & Society*, 24(2), 213–233.

17 Hardensein, L. (2017). The Retirement Wisdom Podcast. Creating Your Second Act Career. https://www.retirementwisdom.com/podcasts/creating-your-second-act-career-linda-hardenstein/.

18 Jarvis, C. (2019). *Creative Calling*. Harper Collins, p. 40.

19   Javie, S. (2020, June). From the NBA Hardwood to the Altar. The Retirement Wisdom podcast. https://www.retirementwisdom.com/podcasts/from-the-nba-hardwood-to-the-altar-steve-javie/.

20   Davey, M. (2020, October). What Do You Really Want to Do? The Retirement Wisdom podcast. https://www.retirementwisdom.com/podcasts/what-do-you-really-want-to-do-melissa-davey/.

CHAPTER TEN

1   Dennis, H. (2019, November 25). Advice for Successful Career Women Transitioning to Retirement. The Retirement Wisdom Podcast. https://www.retirementwisdom.com/podcasts/advice-for-successful-career-women-transitioning-to-retirement-helen-dennis/.

2   Emmons, R. A., & Mishra, A. (2011). Why Gratitude Enhances Well-Being: What We Know, What We Need to Know. Designing Positive Psychology: Taking Stock and Moving Forward, 248–262.

3   Seligman, M. E. P., Steen, T. A., Park, N., & Peterson, C. (2005). Positive Psychology Progress: Empirical Validation of Interventions. American Psychologist, 60, 410–421.

4   Emmons & Mishra (2011), p. 249.

5   Emmons & Mishra (2011), pp. 250–251.

6   Tung, L. (2019, November 21). Your Brain on Gratitude: How a Neuroscientist Used His Research to Heal from Grief. PBS. WHYY.org. https://whyy.org/segments/your-brain-on-gratitude-how-a-neuroscientist-used-his-research-to-heal-from-grief/.

7   Fox, G. R., Kaplan, J., Damasio, H., & Damasio, A. (2015). Neural Correlates of Gratitude. Frontiers in Psychology, 6, 1491.

8   Tung (2019).

9   Seligman et al. (2005).

10   Emmons (2013), p. 12.

11   Toepfer, S. M., & Walker, K. (2009, Nov.). Letters of Gratitude: Improving Well-Being Through Expressive Writing. Journal of Writing Research, 1(3).

12   Emmons (2013), pp. 5354.

13   Watkins, P. C., Emmons, R. A., Greaves, M. R., & Bell, J. (2018). Joy is a Distinct Positive Emotion: Assessment of Joy and Relationship to Gratitude and Well-Being. The Journal of Positive Psychology, 13(5), 522–539.

14   Merriam-Webster Dictionary. https://www.merriam-webster.com/dictionary/joy.

15   Watkins, P. C. et al. (2018).

16   Hunt, E. (2020, January 1). The Joy Audit: How to Have More Fun in 2020. *The Guardian*. https://www.theguardian.com/lifeandstyle/2020/jan/01/how-to-have-more-fun-in-2020.

17   Lee, I. F. (2018). *Joyful: The Surprising Power of Ordinary Things to Create Extraordinary Happiness*. Ebury Publishing.

18   Martin, R. A., Puhlik-Doris, P., Larsen, G., Gray, J., & Weir, K. (2003). Individual Differences in Uses of Humor and Their Relation to Psychological Well-Being: Development of the Humor Styles Questionnaire. *Journal of Research in Personality*, 37(1), 48–75.

19   Schneider, M., Voracek, M., & Tran, U. S. (2018). "A Joke a Day Keeps the Doctor Away?" Meta-Analytical Evidence of Differential Associations of Habitual Humor Styles with Mental Health. *Scandinavian Journal of Psychology*, 59(3), 289–300.

20   Gibson, JM. (2020, November 23). Laughing is Good for Your Mind and Your Body— Here's What the Research Shows. *TheConversation.com*. https://theconversation.com/laughing-is-good-for-your-mind-and-your-body-heres-what-the-research-shows-145984.

21   Greengross, G. (2013). Humor and Aging—A Mini-Review. *Gerontology*, 59(5), 448–453.

22   Gibson (2020).

CHAPTER ELEVEN

1   Dyer, W. W. (2010). *The Shift*. Hay House, Inc.

2   Benbow, J. (2020, December 22). Remembering Bruce Seals, Who Went from Playing in the NBA/ABA to Changing the Lives of Boston's Kids. *The Boston Globe*. https://www.bostonglobe.com/2020/12/22/sports/bruce-seals-was-steady-consistent-presence-who-helped-changes-lives-bostons-youth/.

3   Colby, A., Remington, K., Bundick, M., Morton, E., Malin, H. & Hirsh, E. (2018). Purpose in the Encore Years: Shaping Lives of Meaning and Contribution. *Encore.org*. https://encore.org/wp-content/uploads/2018/03/PEP-Full-Report.pdf.

4   Hill, P. L., Turiano, N. A., & Burrow, A. L. (2018). Early Life Adversity As a Predictor of Sense of Purpose During Adulthood. *International Journal of Behavioral Development*, 42(1), 143–147.

5   *One-Third of Your Life Is Spent at Work: The Average Person Will Spend 90,000 Hours at Work Over a Lifetime*. (2020, December.) Gettysburg.edu. Retrieved from https://www.gettysburg.edu/news/stories?id=79db7b34-630c-4f49-ad32-4ab9ea48e72b#:~:text=Writer%20Annie%20Dillard%20famously%20said,at%20work%20over%20a%20lifetime.

6   Maestas, N., Mullen, K. J., Powell, D., Von Wachter, T., & Wenger, J. B. (2017). *Working Conditions in the United States: Results of the 2015 American Working Conditions Survey*. Santa Monica, CA: RAND Corporation.

7 Maestas, N., Mullen, K. J., Powell, D., von Wachter, T., & Wenger, J. B. (2019). The American Working Conditions Survey Finds that Nearly Half of Retirees Would Return to Work. RAND Corporation, 2019. https://www.rand.org/pubs/research_briefs/RB9973-1.html.

8 *The Four Pillars of the New Retirement.* (2020, August 4). EdwardJones.com. Retrieved from agewave.com/the-four-pillars-of-the-new-retirement.

9 *Planning for the 30+ Year Retirement.* (2020). Stanford Center on Longevity and Wells Fargo Wealth Management. WellsFargo.com. Retrieved from https://www08.wellsfargomedia.com/assets/pdf/personal/the-private-bank/The_30-Plus_Year_Retirement_paper.pdf.

10 Hill, P. L., & Turiano, N. A. (2014). Purpose in Life as a Predictor of Mortality Across Adulthood. *Psychological Science, 25*(7), 1482–1486.

11 Cole, D. (2013, January 13). Why You Need to Find a Mission: Having a Purpose in Life, New Research Shows, Could Be the Key to a Successful Retirement. *The Wall Street Journal.* https://www.wsj.com/articles/SB10001424127887323316804578163501792318298; Boyle, P. A., Buchman, A. S., Barnes, L. L., & Bennett, D. A. (2010). Effect of a Purpose in Life on Risk of Incident Alzheimer's Disease and Mild Cognitive Impairment in Community-Dwelling Older Persons. *Archives of General Psychiatry, 67*(3), 304–310.

12 Kaplin, A., & Anzaldi, L. (2015). New Movement in Neuroscience: A Purpose-Driven Life. *Cerebrum: The Dana Forum on Brain Science, 2015,* 7.

13 Steptoe, A., & Fancourt, D. (2019). Leading a Meaningful Life at Older Ages and its Relationship with Social Engagement, Prosperity, Health, Biology, and Time Use. *Proceedings of the National Academy of Sciences of the United States of America, 116*(4), 1207–1212.

14 Pinquart, M. (2002). Creating and Maintaining Purpose in Life in Old Age: A Meta-Analysis. *Ageing international, 27*(2), 90–114.

15 Alimujiang, A., Wiensch, A., Boss, J., Fleischer, N. L., Mondul, A. M., McLean, K., & Pearce, C. L. (2019). Association Between Life Purpose and Mortality Among US Adults Older than 50 Years. *JAMA Network Open, 2*(5), e194270.

16 Heaven, B., O'Brien, N., Evans, E. H., White, M., Meyer, T. D., Mathers, J. C., & Moffatt, S. (2016). Mobilizing Resources for Well-Being: Implications for Developing Interventions in the Retirement Transition. *The Gerontologist, 56*(4), 615–629.

17 Rapkin, B. D., & Fischer, K. (1992). Framing the Construct of Life Satisfaction in Terms of Older Adults' Personal Goals. *Psychology and Aging, 7*(1), 138 in Osborne, J. W. (2012), p. 49.

18 Heaven et al. (2016), p. 626.

19 Burnett, W., & Evans, D. (2016). *Designing Your Life.* Knopf.

20 Kraemer, H. (2020, December 14). How to Live a Values-Based Life—Harry Kraemer. The Retirement Wisdom Podcast. https://www.retirementwisdom.com/podcasts/how-to-live-a-values-based-life-harry-kraemer/.

21 Kraemer, H. (2020, December 14).

22 *Giving in Retirement: America's Longevity Bonus.* (2015, October 22). Merrill Lynch & Age Wave. https://agewave.com/wp-content/uploads/2016/07/2015-ML-AW-Giving-in-Retirement_Americas-Longevity-Bonus.pdf

23 Carr, D. C., Fried, L. P., & Rowe, J. W. (2015). Productivity & Engagement in an Aging America: The Role of Volunteerism. *Daedalus*, 144(2), 55–67.

24 Dyer (2010).

25 Barnett, C. (2020, May 8). Retired, But Not Done Yet. The Retirement Wisdom Podcast. https://www.retirementwisdom.com/podcasts/retired-but-not-done-yet/.

26 *The Four Pillars of the New Retirement.* (2020, August 4), p. 18.

27 Covey, S. R. (1989). *The 7 Habits of Highly Effective People: An Extraordinary Step-by-Step Guide to Achieving the Human Characteristics that Really Create Success.* Simon and Schuster.

EPILOGUE

28 Covey, S. R. (1989). *The 7 Habits of Highly Effective People: An Extraordinary Step-by-Step Guide to Achieving the Human Characteristics that Really Create Success.* Simon and Schuster.

1 Jackson, M. (2021, January 17). The Gift of Being Unsure of What to Do. *The Boston Globe.* https://www.bostonglobe.com/2021/01/17/opinion/gift-being-unsure-what-do/.

2 Vanderbilt, T. (2021). *Beginners: The Joy and Transformative Power of Lifetime Learning.* Knopf.

3 Brooks, A. C. (2021, January 16.) *Leadership and Happiness. A Special Event with His Holiness, The Dalai Lama.* Harvard Business School class livestreamed. YouTube. https://www.youtube.com/watch?v=akB2qt-WPdg

Made in the USA
Middletown, DE
30 March 2023

27985878R00139